FURY OF THE NORTHMEN

TimeFrame AD 800-1000

THE VIKING WORLD

THE AMERICAS

Time Frame AD 800-1000

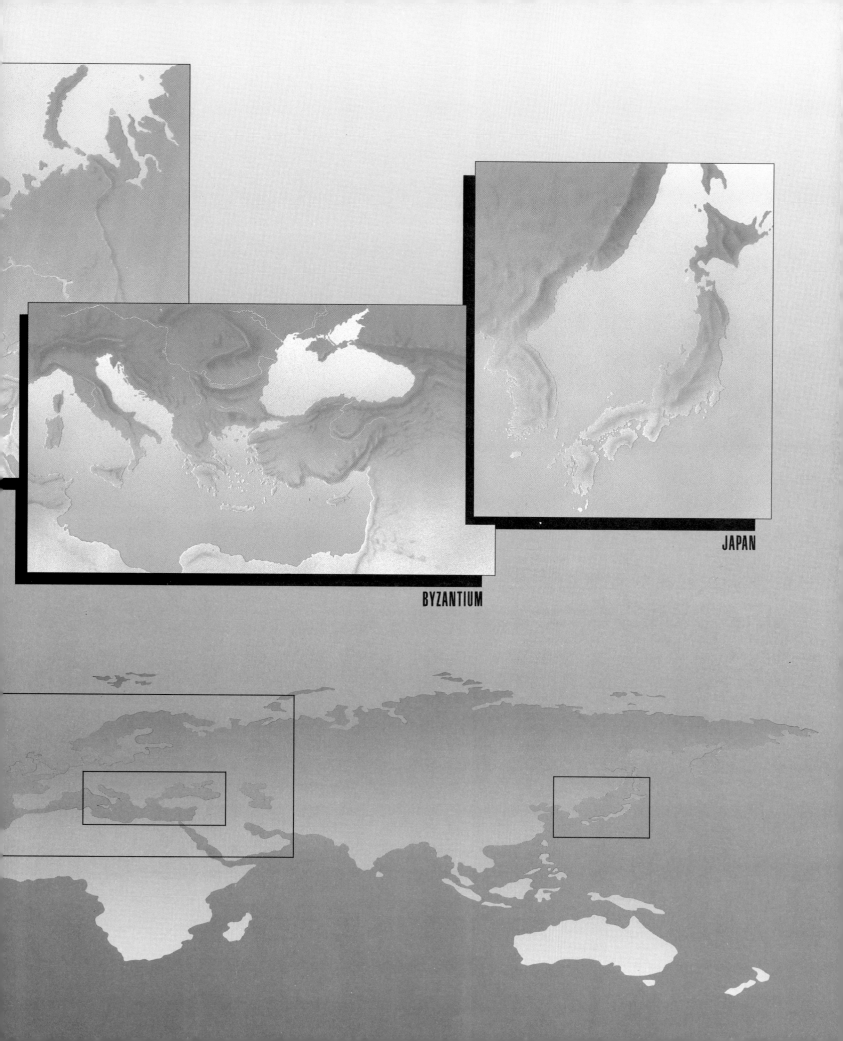

BYZANTIUM

JAPAN

This volume is one in a series that tells the story
of humankind. Other books in the series include:
The Age of God-Kings
Barbarian Tides
A Soaring Spirit
Empires Ascendant
Empires Besieged
The March of Islam

FURY OF THE NORTHMEN

TimeFrame AD 800-1000

BY THE EDITORS OF TIME-LIFE BOOKS

TIME-LIFE BOOKS, ALEXANDRIA, VIRGINIA

Time-Life Books Inc.
is a wholly owned subsidiary of
TIME INCORPORATED

FOUNDER: Henry R. Luce 1898-1967

Editor-in-Chief: Jason McManus
Chairman and Chief Executive Officer:
J. Richard Munro
President and Chief Operating Officer:
N. J. Nicholas, Jr.
Editorial Director: Ray Cave
Executive Vice President, Books:
Kelso F. Sutton
Vice President, Books: George Artandi

TIME-LIFE BOOKS INC.

EDITOR: George Constable
Executive Editor: Ellen Phillips
Director of Design: Louis Klein
Director of Editorial Resources:
Phyllis K. Wise
Editorial Board: Russell B. Adams, Jr.,
Dale M. Brown, Roberta Conlan,
Thomas H. Flaherty, Lee Hassig, Donia
Ann Steele, Rosalind Stubenberg, Henry
Woodhead
Director of Photography and Research:
John Conrad Weiser
Assistant Director of Editorial Resources:
Elise Ritter Gibson

PRESIDENT: Christopher T. Linen
Chief Operating Officer: John M. Fahey, Jr.
Senior Vice Presidents: Robert M.
DeSena, James L. Mercer, Paul R.
Stewart
Vice Presidents: Stephen L. Bair, Ralph J.
Cuomo, Neal Goff, Stephen L. Goldstein,
Juanita T. James, Hallett Johnson III,
Carol Kaplan, Susan J. Maruyama,
Robert H. Smith, Joseph J. Ward
Director of Production Services:
Robert J. Passantino

Editorial Operations
Copy Chief: Diane Ullius
Production: Celia Beattie
Library: Louise D. Forstall

Correspondents: Elisabeth Kraemer-Singh
(Bonn); Maria Vincenza Aloisi (Paris);
Ann Natanson (Rome). Valuable
assistance was also provided by: Mirka
Gondicas (Athens); Angelica Lemmer
(Bonn); Tina Haselton, Barbara Gevene
Hertz (Copenhagen); Brendan Keenan
(Dublin); Lance Keyworth (Helsinki); Ara
Güler, Suna Güler (Istanbul); Caroline
Alcock, Caroline Lucas, Linda Proud
(London); Trini Bandrés (Madrid); Felix
Rosenthal (Moscow); Christina
Lieberman (New York); Dag Christensen
(Oslo); Ann Wise (Rome); Mary Johnson
(Stockholm); Dick Berry, Alison
Hashimoto, Mieko Ikeda (Tokyo); Traudl
Lessing (Vienna).

TIME FRAME

SERIES DIRECTOR: Henry Woodhead
Series Administrator:
Philip Brandt George

Editorial Staff for *Fury of the Northmen:*
Designer: Tom Huestis
Associate Editors: Jim Hicks (text); Robin
Richman (pictures)
Writer: Stephen G. Hyslop
Researchers: Patricia McKinney (text);
Oobie Gleysteen, Trudy Pearson,
Barbara Sause (pictures)
Assistant Designers: Rebecca Mowrey,
Alan Pitts
Copy Coordinator: Jarelle S. Stein
Picture Coordinator: Robert H.
Wooldridge, Jr.
Editorial Assistant: Lona Tavernise

Special Contributors: Ronald H. Bailey,
Champ Clark, George G. Daniels,
Thomas A. Lewis, Nancy Lorince, David
S. Thomson, Bryce Walker (text);
Barbara Cohn, Roxie France-Nuriddin,
Ann-Louise G. Gates, Feroline Burrage
Higginson, Evelyn Savage Prettyman,
Jared Rosenfeld, Jacqueline Shaffer,
Susan Sivard (research); Roy Nanovic
(index)

CONSULTANTS

The Americas:
LINDA CORDELL, Irvine Curator and
Chairman of Anthropology, California
Academy of Sciences, San Francisco,
California

GORDON FRANCIS McEWAN, Assistant
Curator, Pre-Columbian Collection,
Dumbarton Oaks, Washington, D.C.

BRUCE SMITH, Curator of North Ameri-
can Archeology, National Museum of
Natural History, Smithsonian Institution,
Washington, D.C.

Byzantium:
MARIE TAYLOR DAVIS, Assistant Professor, Department of Foreign Languages
and Literatures, George Mason University, Fairfax, Virginia

ALICE-MARY TALBOT, Executive Editor,
Oxford Dictionary of Byzantium, Dumbarton Oaks, Washington, D.C.

Japan:
ROBERT BORGEN, Associate Professor
and Chairman of the Department of East
Asian Languages and Literature, Univer-
sity of Hawaii, Manoa, Honolulu,
Hawaii

Scandinavia and the Vikings:
RICHARD RINGLER, Professor of English
and Scandinavian Studies, Department of
Scandinavian Studies, University of Wisconsin, Madison, Wisconsin

LENA THÅLIN-BERGMAN, Archeologist,
Statens Historiska Museum, Stockholm,
Sweden

PATRICK F. WALLACE, Assistant Keeper,
Irish Antiquities Division, National Museum of Ireland, Dublin, Ireland

**Library of Congress Cataloging in
Publication Data**

Fury of the Northmen.
  Bibliography: p.
  Includes index.
  1. Middle Ages—History. I. Time-Life Books.
D123.F87 1988   909.07   87-33585
ISBN 0-8094-6425-X
ISBN 0-8094-6426-8 (lib. bdg.)

Time-Life Books Inc. offers a wide range of fine
recordings, including a *Rock 'n' Roll Era* series.
For subscription information, call 1-800-621-
7026 or write Time-Life Music, P.O. Box C-
32068, Richmond, Virginia 23261-2068.

CONTENTS

THE VIKING ONSLAUGHT

1

The year 793 began ominously for the people of Northumbria in northeastern Britain. There were "immense whirlwinds and flashes of lightning," according to contemporary accounts, "and fiery dragons were seen flying in the air." To the chroniclers, these were portents of the terror that followed, cosmic signs of impending sacrilege.

The disaster struck that year at Lindisfarne off the Northumbrian coast. Lonely and windswept, Lindisfarne was home only to the monks of St. Cuthbert's monastery. It was undefended, and perhaps people thought it needed no defense: Lindisfarne was the Holy Island, revered as the first seat of Christianity in Britain. Its monastery had stood for more than 150 years.

On June 8 of this year, however, square sails flashed on the North Sea horizon, and the ships that bore them—long, low ships with high curving prows and sterns—sped across the waters and rammed onto Lindisfarne's beaches, disgorging a horde of ruddy, shouting warriors, big, savage men who swarmed across the sand and up the island's grassy slopes to the monastery. There they wrought havoc, hacking their way into chapels and storerooms and killing as they went. They were after St. Cuthbert's treasures: illuminated manuscripts bound with jeweled covers, golden crucifixes, silver communion vessels. When at last they finished looting, they took not only gold and gems but monks to be sold into slavery. They left the monastery a smoldering ruin. Its shrines were wrecked, according to one chronicler, and "the bodies of saints trampled like dung in the streets."

These raiders were master sailors, fierce fighters, and greedy looters. During the next decades they struck again and again throughout Europe. In 794, they raided Jarrow on the Tyne River, the monastery where the Venerable Bede, Britain's first historian, had worked. In 795, they attacked St. Columba's on the island of Iona, as well as remote monasteries on Inishbofin and Inishmurray off the west coast of Ireland. In 799, they took St. Philibert's on Noirmoutier at the mouth of the Loire River, which they were to use as a base for inland attacks. By the 840s, they were striking deep into France—into Rouen, into Nantes (where in 843 they murdered the bishop at the altar of his own cathedral), into Chartres, Amiens, Tours, Orléans, Paris. They robbed so many churches and monasteries that a later chronicler was led to write—perhaps apocryphally—that a new prayer had been added to the Christian litany: "From the fury of the Northmen, O, Lord, deliver us."

The Northmen came from Norway, Denmark, and Sweden, but to their many victims they shared one name—a variation of Norsemen. These Scandinavians shared also a common language, way of life, pagan religion, and above all, a predilection for going to sea to raid or trade. It was this last trait that suddenly propelled the Scandinavians into prominence between AD 800 and 1000 under a name—derived perhaps from a Norse word for inlet because they were sailors and perhaps from a word for battle because they were fighters—by which history would know them best. They were called the Vikings.

To be sure, other cultures came into their own during this era. The realm of the Franks, who controlled the western European wing of the old Roman Empire, reached its zenith before plummeting into decline after the death of Charlemagne in 814. Farther east, those other heirs of the Roman Empire, the Byzantines, entered a second golden age, which saw them regain territories lost to the Arabs and achieve new heights in art and literature. In the Far East, the Japanese ushered in the Heian period, absorbing Chinese culture and turning it into something unique. And in the Americas, remarkable cities took shape under civilizations such as the Mississippian mound builders, the Toltec of Mexico, and the Tiahuanacans of Peru.

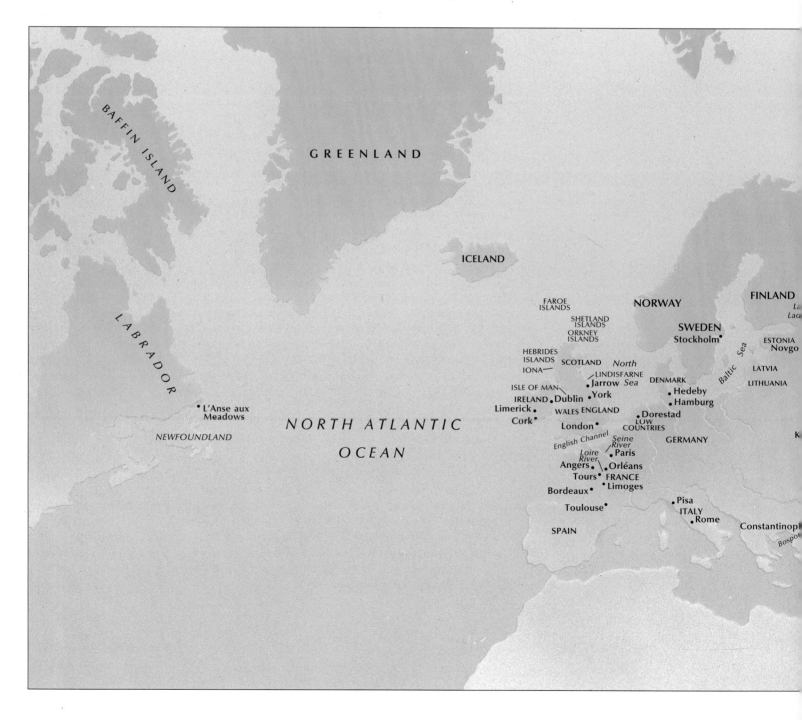

But in raw vitality and breadth of impact, none of these cultures could match that of the Vikings. Driven by greed, the need for trade and land, and the lust for fame, the Vikings reached out with a vengeance during the last two centuries of the first millennium. Though relatively few in number—probably no more than two million people lived in Scandinavia at the dawn of the ninth century—they changed the face of Europe as they moved from trading and raiding to conquest and settlement. They revitalized European commerce and established their own European domains. They extended their civilization into the New World and shed Scandinavian blood—or infused it into the local peoples—over an unprecedented span of the earth from Russia to America.

Each of the evolving Viking nationalities staked out its own sphere of action, determined partly by geography. The Swedes, whose shores faced east, were primarily traders. They moved eastward, sailing the Baltic and then sweeping down the great rivers of Central Europe, deep into Russia, and to Constantinople, the capital of the Byzantine Empire. The Danes worked the North Sea and the English Channel, terrorizing England and France and settling large regions in both. The Norwegians ventured north, southwest, and west. After raids on England's east coast they concentrated on the areas around the Irish Sea, Scotland, and the nearby islands and then challenged uncharted waters to colonize the Faroe Islands, Iceland, and Greenland.

Wherever they ventured, the Vikings took their own ways of life, which were remarkably similar considering the differences among their homelands. The countries of Scandinavia stretched over a formidable distance—1,200 miles from northernmost to southernmost. Geographically, they showed a diversity that varied from the low-lying plains of Denmark and southern Sweden to Norway's mountainous spine and fjord-pierced western coast. Everywhere, Scandinavian life was centered on farming, hunting, and fishing and focused on the family. Home might be an isolated homestead or a small community that typically brought together all the members of one or more extended families.

This agrarian society, like those in most of Europe, comprised three social groups: slaves, freemen, and nobility. The social structure rested to a certain degree upon the thralls, or slaves. They did the heaviest work and were regarded as personal chattel; like an aged or injured horse or dog, they could be put down at their owner's will. Slaves got that way by being captured at home or overseas, or as punishment for indebtedness or certain crimes, or by being born into thralldom. Practically every Scandinavian farm had its slaves. Law dictated that any farm large enough to accommodate twelve cows and two horses should have at least three slaves. A large estate might require thirty or more.

Freemen, a broad and varied social group, formed the center of Scandinavian society. They might be literally freed men—manumitted slaves—for the Scandinavian social structure permitted upward mobility. Slaves could purchase their freedom, and many owners encouraged this by setting aside plots of land for them to work for their own profit. The price of freedom varied: In some parts of Scandinavia, slaves became free only when they staged a feast, an elaborate ceremony at which they served a great quantity of ale—brewed from a specified measure of malt—and provided their old masters with a certain amount of silver. Most freemen were simply born free.

From this group came the Norsemen's fishermen, shipwrights, metalworkers, carpenters, and other craftsmen. Among the freemen, too, were many farm workers. But

the strongest and richest were the *boendr*—literally, those who stayed in one place. These were the landowning farmers. Their fierce independence showed one way Scandinavian society differed from the rest of Europe. A bondi was unencumbered by the dues or duties to an overlord that characterized the feudalism developing elsewhere. The boendr and their fellow freemen were those who in the sailing season—spring and summer—went a-Viking in search of plunder.

The boendr formed alliances, however, usually led by the richest, strongest landholders, who made up Scandinavia's nobility. These wealthy chieftains, who often went by the title of jarl—the source for the English "earl"—included local leaders whose authority might be limited to a single fjord and men who commanded followers from entire provinces, as well as the kings who ruled larger regions and eventually, the Scandinavian nations.

Knitting these various groups loosely together was an old and remarkable system of government and law. Every freeman met periodically with his neighbors in a public assembly known as the Thing. The Thing served as a rudimentary parliament for the making of laws and as a court for trying infringements. Each local community or district had its own Thing, and each of these was part of successively larger groupings—first, by province, then by region or small kingdom. Each larger jurisdiction had an assembly made up of representatives from the local Things. These assemblies, in addition to dealing with matters of law and mutual defense, had the power to approve the selection of jarls or kings.

In theory, the system guided by the Thing represented a significant thrust toward democracy. In everyday practice, however, local and regional chieftains exerted decisive control. It was these leaders who were largely responsible for the evolution of rudimentary nation-states in Scandinavia. Several of them, with the approval of the local Things, would select a kind of regional king. The strongest of these kings would then impose his authority upon fellow monarchs. Through this process, a capable or forceful leader would bring together a number of regions and eventually emerge as sovereign of something resembling a nation. The first Viking monarch to unite a country was Harald Fairhair. King of the province of Vestfold in southeastern Norway, Harald began his ascendancy during the 870s. According to legend, he vowed not to cut his blond hair until he had put down some contentious local chieftains who disputed his right to rule. Strong-willed and energetic, Harald did not stop there but went on to gain control of neighboring provinces through a combination of shrewd diplomacy and vigorous warfare. Sometime around 885, a confederacy of jarls and petty kings who refused to submit to Harald were vanquished in a battle at sea near Hafrs Fjord on the southwestern coast. Only then was Harald recognized as king of all Norway. It would be a century or more before the disparate regions of Norway's sister countries united—Denmark under Svein Forkbeard in 985 and Sweden under Olaf Skautkonung in 993.

All during this period, the Thing legislated daily as well as political life. The laws it pronounced were committed to memory and transmitted by mouth. (No written law code existed in Scandinavia until about 1100.) These laws ran the gamut, from settlements over property boundaries and decisions about whether wooing away a farmer's bees was legal to rulings on offenses considered more serious, such as sheep stealing and murder. But the Thing devoted the most time to keeping the lid on the greatest disturber of the peace in Scandinavian society: blood feuds.

Quarrels between individuals almost always brought in the entire family. An insult

Wealthy Vikings showcased their status through the superior quality of their clothes, jewelry, and weapons. This well-to-do chief, his hair and his beard neatly trimmed, wears a fine woolen cape, secured at the shoulder with a brooch, over a handsome tunic. Close at hand, even in this moment of domestic tranquillity, are the symbols of a Viking warrior's trade: helmet, circular wooden shield, knife, sword with ornamental silver hilt—and purse for valuables. His lady, with her elegant brooches, necklaces, and bracelets keeps her shawl thrown back to display her fair arms. Dangling from a chain is a key for her cupboards and chests.

to one member of the family was considered an insult to all, and minor disputes often escalated into full-scale feuds marked by maimings and killings and endless rounds of retaliation. A family, if it chose, could often stop the escalation of violence by paying compensation to the family of someone it had harmed. This payment of atonement, called *bot,* was then divided among the members of the wronged family.

Adversaries in a blood feud could also bring the matter before the Thing. They and other litigants would then face a group of judges consisting of all the assembly's members or perhaps a smaller panel chosen by the Thing. A defendant, in addition to calling witnesses to testify, could attempt to bolster his case by submitting to trial by ordeal. For example, he might volunteer to hold a handful of red-hot iron scraps for a few terrible seconds. His burn was then bandaged and examined by the jury four days later. If jury members deemed the wound clean, they pronounced him innocent. But if it was festering, they found him guilty and meted out punishment that, depending upon the crime, ranged from payment of a fine to hanging or beheading.

The worst penalty short of death was permanent outlawry—a sentence that left the defendant, in the words of one law, "as if he were dead." He forfeited all his goods and all his legal rights. Anyone could murder him without risk of penalty. For the man thus condemned, the only reasonable recourse was to flee his homeland or hide in the forest and live as an outlaw in fact as well as name.

What supported this violent society was the land and the sea. The Norsemen were farmers first of all, but they depended on a varying mixture of crops, animal husbandry, fishing, and hunting. Agriculture was dominant in the milder south. Turning the soil with the ard—a simple metal point dragged through the dirt—or with the more efficient plow, and harvesting with wood and iron sickles and scythes, farmers grew barley, oats and rye, peas, hops, and cabbages for eating, and flax for making linen. Everywhere the people depended on livestock such as sheep, cattle, goats, and pigs for food as well as wool, skin, bone, and horn. The work was hard because of the climate. Crops could fail. As winter came, weaker animals had to be slaughtered and their meat smoked or salted with salt laboriously made by boiling seawater.

Yet Scandinavia was rich in wild plants and animals, and all the people added gathering, hunting, and fishing to their farming. Among the wild fare to be had were apples, elderberries, blackberries, and blueberries, not to mention hazelnuts and walnuts, garlic and leeks. The seas and lakes teemed with fish; whales could be driven into shallow inlets and slaughtered. Walrus and seal were plentiful, and there were seabirds to be netted and ducks and grouse to be shot.

For hunting, too, there were reindeer, red deer, bears, and rabbits. These provided not only food but antler and bone for household tools such as knife handles and spindle whorls. And successful hunters had goods to trade: furs for instance, as well as seal, bear, and reindeer skin, not to mention treasures such as walrus ivory.

Farmers, fishermen, huntsmen, traders, the early Norsemen were country people, not townsfolk, who lived sometimes in small villages but more often in remote and widely scattered farmsteads. When prosperous, these holdings might form small communities in themselves.

The hub of such a farm was the longhouse, or hall house, where everyone—master, mistress, children, craftsmen, laborers, and slaves—ate and slept. Rectangular structures that might be as long as 100 feet, these houses were variously built from timber, stone, wattle and daub, or even sod. Windows, if any, would be small, covered with wooden shutters during cold weather and sometimes with panes made of polished horn. The only other openings to the outside were doors and smoke holes in the roofs.

A longhouse might be divided into two or three rooms—the smaller ones used as storerooms or as byres—but its heart was the central hall. The floor of the hall was earth, sometimes covered with a carpet of reeds; a long pit that served as the hearth ran along the center, and the walls were lined with wood-covered earthen benches for sitting and sleeping. Other furnishings were simple. The center section of one wall bench was the rightful seat of the owner, marked by ornately carved flanking pillars, which apparently were movable, since settlers took them on voyages of exploration. Against one wall in most houses stood an upright, warp-weighted loom. On other walls hung weapons and various tools. Near the hearth were stacks of soapstone, pottery, and wooden vessels for cooking and storage. Clothes were kept in wooden chests and so, presumably, was the bedding—straw-stuffed mattresses, woolen blankets, coverings of skins and furs—that was used to make the wall benches into beds.

Life in the longhouse was crowded, busy, and dark. Women cooked the morning and evening meals at one end of the long hearth, baking bread of unleavened barley flour on a flat stone, cooking porridge, soup, and stewed meats in pots set nearby. Meat was roasted on iron or wooden spits set over the fire. (The English word "steak" is related to the Old Norse *steikja*, meaning "to roast on a spit.") Cooking, and the fact that the hearth fire was never allowed to go out, meant that the hall was smoky. Besides hearth light, the people had only oil lamps for illumination. Outside the longhouse were other buildings. Sometimes there were bathhouses, forerunners of steambaths. There were sheds, byres, and barns, and if the farmer lived by the sea, he would have a house for storing his boat during the cold months.

Men were masters of their farms, but the symbol of capable authority and domestic order was the housewife with her keys at her waist. A woman's legal position was not strong. She remained in the care of her father or guardian until a suitable marriage was arranged for her, and after the payment of her dowry and bride-price, she passed into her husband's charge. His powers were great: He could keep a concubine; he could kill an adulterous wife and her lover; he could order a sickly infant put to death. Yet women as well as men could seek divorce by declaring before witnesses the grounds—impotence, for example. Women could own land. Widows, especially, by inheriting their husband's property, could become wealthy and powerful landowners. And women ran the households and dairies both when their husbands were at home and during the long months of absence when the men were away seafaring. It was no wonder that foreigners commented on the independent behavior of the Norse women they encountered.

Like the men, the women loved finery. This was a people fond of display. Their clothing—its wool or linen fabric spun and woven by the housewives—was adapted to the extreme climate: for men, shirts and underbreeches, sashed or belted trousers, and tunics held by belts for knives and purses; for women, short-sleeved chemises, gartered hose, long flowing overdresses, and shawls. Both sexes wore enveloping cloaks and mittens, gloves and hats of wool or fur.

The clothes were the background—among those who could afford it—for spectacular ornamentation. Women's overdresses were pinned by paired brooches, and a third brooch held their shawls in place. Men and women alike wore finger rings, arm rings, and necklaces, and these pieces, signs of wealth and successful trade or looting, often were of breathtaking magnificence. They were cast from gold and silver, twisted into sinuous chains or shaped into the most delicate filigrees that were interlaced in abstract or animal shapes of dazzling complexity. A rich man's neck ring might be made of heavily braided pure gold. His sword belt, his drinking cup, his horse's collar, and his ship's weathervane might be gilded and enriched with filigree, too, for decoration was not limited to jewelry. The jewelry might be designed just to glitter in the light. And the glitter was not confined to precious metals. Scandinavian jewelry gleamed with colored glass and with amber, crystal, and carnelian.

In the splendor of their jewels and the crudeness of their houses, in the strength of their family loyalties and the savagery of their attacks on their European neighbors, the pagan Norse seemed a people of barbarian extremes. Indeed, they were bred in lands of extremes, both in geography and in climate. There was fertile country from the north to the south of Scandinavia, but the good land faced vast stretches of inimical wastes. Low-lying Denmark had wildernesses of bogs and heaths and miles of drifting, sandy coasts. Its many islands were dominated by cold and often stormy seas. Sweden had huge tracks of bog, dense forests, and mountainous areas, as did Norway. The region was cold. Southern Sweden, for instance, was snow covered as much as sixty days a year; farther north, snow might stay on the ground for four months. Lakes would be frozen from November to April in some areas. Parts of the Baltic were ice locked for three months of the year. And with the cold came darkness—especially in the most northerly regions, where in deep winter, the sun barely appeared for months.

The beliefs of the pagan Norse were shaped by this harsh environment. Theirs was a pantheistic religion, variable in its tenets and practices, that reflected the world they knew. In the beginning, they thought, there was a void—an emptiness of mist and frost. A primal giant called Ymir arose from this, and from him was born a race of frost giants, the most ancient of gods. Almost all the frost giants were killed by their own descendants. The younger gods made the earth from Ymir's body and set it in the midst of a girdling ocean. At its center was Midgard, fortified by high boundary mountains (the name means "boundary wall"). This was where humans lived. In the icy deserts to the north of the mountains was Utgard, where the surviving frost giants were imprisoned. Under Midgard, deep in the earth, was Hel, watched over by a dark goddess of the same name; this was where humans who died of age or sickness went. High above the earth was Asgard, home of the younger gods, who lived in palaces thatched with silver. In Asgard was Valhalla—Hall of the Slain—the glorious heaven where dead human warriors feasted and fought, waiting to return for the last battle, Ragnarok, in which the world would be destroyed by fire and ice.

Of the gods of the living world, chief was Odin, god of the creation, of battles, and of the dead; he was one-eyed, having given an eye as payment for divine wisdom; ravens were his all-seeing scouts in the world of humans. Among his companions—often placed ahead of him—was Thor, god of thunder, ruler of the winds, rains, and crops; his symbol was the hammer. Frey was the god of fruitfulness and fertility; he was a battle god, too, and drove a chariot pulled by a boar with golden bristles. The boar was his sacred animal, sacrificed to him at midwinter festivals. Freya, his sister, was goddess of love. There were scores of lesser gods guarding the elements. Important among them was the fearsome Ran, the "cruel and unfeeling" goddess of the angry sea, who craved the souls of the drowned. Below the gods were magic beings, such as dwarfs, who were master artisans, and elves, who dwelled in woodlands and

THE LEGACY OF THE GODS

The Norse tale of creation is related in twenty-nine eleventh-century Icelandic poems known as the Poetic Edda, excerpted here. They say that a clash of fire and frost in the Great Void spawned the giant Ymir, the first living creature, whose sweat begot offspring. Ymir was later killed by Odin and his brothers, who created from the giant's corpse the sky, sea, and earth. Above the earth were the gods' home, Asgard, and Valhalla, where Vikings who died bravely in battle would spend eternity consuming pork and mead and brawling happily among themselves.

But catastrophe lies in store for all when sins beset humankind and bring on a frightful winter. Quakes topple mountains and the old gods are killed in a cataclysmic battle against giants, monsters, fiends, and evil legions from Hel.

Yet an immense ash tree survives, and its branches are haven for two humans who repopulate an earth purified by the holocaust. A new generation of gods is born, and Viking warriors find everlasting contentment in Valhalla.

The loathsome World Serpent coils gracefully upon itself in this seventh-century brooch from Sweden. In Norse mythology, the reptile frequently stirred up tempests by lashing the sea with its tail. Bursting from its oceanic lair for the climactic doomsday of the gods, or Ragnarok, the snake would be slain by Thor, who would then take nine steps and fall dead of its venom.

When Ymir lived,
    Long ages ago,
Before there were seas,
    Chill waves or shore,
Earth was not yet
    Nor the high heavens
But a great emptiness
    Nowhere green.

Then all the gods
  Met to give judgment,
The holy gods
  Took counsel together:
They named night
  And the waning moon,
They gave names
  To morning and midday,
Afternoon and evening,
  Ordered time by years.

There is an ash tree—
  Its name is Yggdrasil—
A tall tree sparkling
  With clear drops of dew
Which fall from its boughs
  Down into the valleys;
Ever green it stands
  Beside the Norns' spring.

And in Asgard
  Gold-Comb crowed,
The cock who wakes
  Odin's warriors;
Another is heard
  Below the Earth,
A soot-red cock
  In the halls of Hel.

Many spells I know,
  And I can see
The doom that awaits
  The almighty gods.

Brothers will die,
  Slain by their brothers,
Incest will break
  Kinship's bonds;
Woe to the world then,
  Wedded to whoredom,
Battle-axe and sword rule,
  Split shields asunder,
Storm-cleft age of wolves
  Until the world goes down,
Only hatred
  In the hearts of men.

I see rising
  A second time
Out of the waters
  The Earth, green once more;
An eagle flies
  Over rushing waterfalls,
Hunting for fish
  From the craggy heights.

I see a hall
  Fairer than the sun,
Thatched with gold;
  It stands at Gimli.
There shall deserving
  People dwell
To the end of time
  And enjoy their happiness.

Scenes from the Viking
afterlife are depicted in
this pictorial stone from
the Swedish island of Gotland. At top, a warrior arriving on horseback in Valhalla is greeted by a
Valkyrie with a drinking
horn. In the bottom panel,
the two cloaked figures
are probably Vikings sailing to Valhalla—with a
mysterious, dimly seen
stranger above them, per-
haps pointing the way.

Odin's heroes
  Know his hall
As soon as they see it;
  Spears are its rafters,
Shields thatch the roof
  Byrnies cover the benches.

Odin's heroes
  Know his hall
As soon as they see it;
  A wolf hangs over
The western door,
  Above it an eagle hovers.

Guarding Valhalla
  A holy gate
Defends the inner doors;
  Ancient it is,
And few men know
  What kind of lock will close it.

Five hundred
  And forty doors
You will find in Valhalla;
  Eight hundred warriors
Will use just one
  When they go to fight Fenrir.

The valiant warriors
  Who wait in Valhalla
Fight to the death each day;
  They bring the slain
Back from the battle,
  Then they all sit in peace again.

grassy mounds. And as in other pagan societies, the things of nature—mountains, streams, trees—had their own spirits to guard them.

The other spirits thought to walk the earth were ghosts: Scandinavians treated death and the dead with great gravity, perhaps to help the deceased on their way to the otherworlds and perhaps to protect themselves from the spirits, for Scandinavian ghosts were ghouls that preyed on living people. Grave sites often were elaborately prepared and furnished. Burial mounds might contain stores of food and household goods such as chairs, beds, and even carts, as well as jewels evidently intended to comfort the deceased in the afterlife. In some instances, a man's wife or female slave was slain to provide him company in death. And to carry him on the voyage into the hereafter, he might be buried in a small rowboat or a seagoing ship.

Other religious practices varied, but the main festivals, presided over not by priests but by chieftains, were tied to the seasons. They were meant to increase safety and fertility, and they were held at midwinter, midsummer, and in the autumn after the harvest. Sacrifice of animals and sometimes of humans played a great part in these ceremonies. So bloody could the rituals be that a later chronicler wrote of sacred groves hung with corpses of dogs, horses, and men. The examination of oracles—lots marked with animals' blood—might accompany the rites. Wild feasting followed. To establish communion among gods and humans, the slaughtered animals were eaten.

An important feature of such festivals and of Scandinavian life in general was the emphasis on the chanted or spoken word. To the Norse, words had god-given magic power—the source of skill and art was Odin. The Norsemen used their hours at the feast fire to give genealogies and to tell tales of gods and men. Poets cast the words into complex verse with rigid patterns of alliteration and internal rhyme.

If the Scandinavians recorded their poems and stories in writing during the ninth and tenth centuries, virtually none survived. They wrote in runes, an ancient alphabet derived in large part from Latin and other southern European alphabets. Runes during the Viking era consisted of sixteen phonetic letters, each of which served both as a unit in a word and as the name for an object or concept central to Scandinavian life. Runes were imbued with magic: They were another gift of the wise god Odin. The very word derives from the Old Norse *run*, meaning mystery.

Runes were designed especially for inscribing in wood or stone. Each letter consisted of simple straight strokes suitable for inscriptions but difficult and cumbersome for transcribing running text. Not until the eleventh century did Scandinavians adopt easier ways of writing the histories and tales of their ancestors and gods.

Beyond all other factors shaping their lives, however—their land, the pagan religion, the government, the farms—Scandinavians were most profoundly affected by the sea. From the earliest times, they had plied the fjords, rivers, and lakes of their homelands to fish and trade. Even the hostile, more than 1,600-mile-long western coast of Norway was conducive to local seafaring because of the clusters of little islands—150,000 in all—that created a protective breakwater against the gale-swept Atlantic. During the eighth century, advances in shipbuilding transformed the people from coastal sailors into true Vikings. At that time, shipwrights learned to add large masts and sails to their ships, which previously had been powered by oars. This, in turn, spurred the development of a keel strong enough to provide stability. These developments enabled the Vikings to make long voyages over open water.

Scandinavians prized their ships above all other possessions. They lavished on them their finest artwork—awesome figureheads and exquisitely designed ornamental trim—and some of their most vivid prose and poetry. "Here there were glittering men of solid gold or silver nearly comparable to live ones, there bulls with necks raised high and legs outstretched were fashioned leaping and roaring like live ones," observed one chronicler. And watching the ships depart, he wrote, "The blue water, smitten by many oars, might be seen foaming far and wide, and the sunlight, cast back in the gleam of metal, spread a double radiance in the air."

No less an art than shipbuilding was the remarkable skill with which Viking navigators plotted their courses in the open sea, a skill developed through centuries of intimacy with the ocean. Viking mariners knew how to read nautical phenomena—from the flight of birds and the movements of other sea creatures to the attributes of the ocean itself, such as color, temperature, and currents—in order to learn where they were. Lacking a magnetic compass, they took their bearings by using crude instruments to sight the Sun and Polaris, the North Star.

The first major thrust of the Viking era involved trading rather than raiding. The Swedes, facing the Baltic, crossed that body of water during the eighth century to establish trading posts in southern Finland and in present-day Latvia, Lithuania, and Estonia. Going abroad to trade was nothing new for Scandinavians. At least since 1500 BC, intrepid merchants had loaded small, crude boats with commodities such as amber—the fossilized resin of ancient pine trees that was valued as jewelry for its golden hue—and rowed down the rivers of western Europe, venturing as far as Ireland and Britain to barter for gold, copper, and tin. Over the centuries new exports were added, most notably the valuable yield from the great northern animals: furs and hides for cloaks and other outerwear, ivory from walrus tusks for crucifixes and caskets, strips of sealskin for ship's cables.

In the early ninth century, drawn farther eastward into Russia by the lure of silver, the Swedes sailed into Lake Ladoga and then turned south into the river routes of that vast land. At Staraya Ladoga, a few miles south of the lake, and at Novgorod, about 100 miles farther on, the intruders established important trading posts. The local Slavs referred to them as Rus, possibly a corruption of the Finnish word for Swedes, Ruotsi, and perhaps the source of Russia's very name.

From this region, Viking traders took two major river routes. One led south down the Dnieper into an area where they established a major trading town at another Slavic settlement, Kiev. From Kiev, these Vikings and their Rus descendants rowed on to the Black Sea and along its western shore into the Byzantine Empire's capital, Constantinople. Some had conquest in mind. Beginning in 860, the Rus mounted a century-long series of unsuccessful attacks against Constantinople.

The other river route led eastward on the Volga into the land of the Bulgars. Near the town of Bulgar, the Volga bent south, flowed through the area controlled by Khazars, and then onward to the Caspian Sea. Vikings sailed the length of the Caspian and rode about 400 miles by camel to the ancient city of Baghdad, where they traded for such eastern exotica as spices from India and silk from China. More commonly, Viking merchants received silver in exchange for their goods. Because Scandinavians did not mint coins in any quantity until about 975, these early traders treated foreign silver coins as bullion. They weighed them out on the portable scales that virtually every Viking trader carried. To achieve an exact weight, merchants often cut the coins into halves, quarters, or even smaller fragments, which became known as hacksilver.

Vikings on the Volga route accumulated a vast store of silver coins from Arab

ᚴᛅᚢᛚᚠᛦ	ᛅᚢᚴ	ᛅᚢᛏᛁᛦ	ᚦᛅᛦ	ᛋᛅᚢᛏᚢ
kaulfR	auk	autiR	þaR	sautu
Kaulfr	and	Autir	they	put

ᛋᛏᛅᛁᚾ	ᚦᛅᚾᛋᛁ	ᛅᚠᛏᛁᛦ	ᛏᚢᛘᛅ	ᛒᚱᚢᚦᚢᚱ
stain	þansj	aftiR	tuma	bruþur
stone	this	after	Tumi	brother

ᛋᛁᛅ	ᛁᛦ	ᛅᛏᛁ	ᚴᚢᚦᛁᛋᛋᚾᛅᛒᚾ
sia	iR	ati	kuþissnabn
their	who	owned	Gusnava.

entrepreneurs operating northward from Persia and other Muslim-held territories in the Near East. What the Arabs wanted most of all, and what the Vikings provided in abundance, were human slaves. Slaves were in demand practically everywhere, of course, and few people—not even their own compatriots—were safe from the Viking clutches. "As soon as one has caught his neighbor," wrote a German chronicler, "he sells him ruthlessly as a slave, to either friend or stranger." Vast numbers of slaves were simply bought or captured by Viking raiders in western and central Europe, however. Before these regions converted to Christianity, they provided a large supply—from the sale of prisoners, debtors, and criminals. The Church tried to cut off the trade, not because the bishops objected to slavery, but because they did not like the idea of Christians being owned by the infidel Muslims. In northern Russia, too, Vikings found a mother lode for the Arabs among the Slavic tribes. They swooped down upon the Slavic settlements and took as tribute or plunder so many people to be sold into bondage that Slav later became the root of the word "slave."

Many of the Rus stayed on in Russia and played an important part in the foundation of its early medieval city-states. Their Scandinavian ways soon merged into the prevailing Slavic culture. Other Vikings became mercenary soldiers for the Byzantine Empire, forming the famed Varangian elite guard in Constantinople. Still others continued to work the river routes that led back to the Baltic and thus homeward with their bounty of slaves, silk, and spices, and purses full of silver.

Trade with the East, as well as with the British Isles and western Europe, stimulated the growth of what may have been Scandinavia's first true towns, market centers that rose to prominence around 800. All these towns were near major trade routes; natural and man-made defenses protected them from rival Vikings.

Consider, for example, the town of Birka, the major port for goods coming via the Volga route in Russia. Birka was situated on the island of Björök ("Birch Island") in Lake Mälar, some eighteen miles west of the site of present-day Stockholm, which in turn lay thirty miles inland from the Baltic Sea via a labyrinth of islands and reefs. The town, covering an area of about thirty acres, was enclosed by a semicircular earthen rampart topped by a palisade. To the south of Birka rose a 100-foot-high fortified outcropping of stone, which commanded the approaches to the town and served as a refuge in time of danger. And to further protect the foreign traders there—the Frisians, Danes, Germans, Finns, and other merchants who appeared during the summer trading months—the Swedes seem to have maintained a garrison and made an exception to the law that exempted the killing of foreigners from penalty.

The largest and oldest Viking town was the Danish port of Hedeby, where several major trade routes intersected. Situated on the narrow neck of the Jutland Peninsula, Hedeby was on the Schlei Fjord, some twenty-five miles inland from the Baltic. Hedeby also had access to the North Sea. An overland journey to the west of less than ten miles carried travelers to Hollingstedt on the river Treene, which emptied into the sea, so merchants could avoid the trip through the pirate-infested waters between the Jutland and Scandinavian peninsulas. Hedeby, moreover, was well shielded. A semicircular wall and moat embraced its sixty acres. And to the west, the Danevirke—a nine-mile-long system of ditches and ramparts up to eighteen feet high—defined Denmark's border and defended it against German invaders.

Thriving and, for its time, cosmopolitan, Hedeby was rich in goods both made and traded. Danes made glass, smelted iron, cast bronze, and carved combs and knife

In Norse mythology, the wise god Odin hung for nine nights from a windswept tree to acquire knowledge of the mystic powers possessed by runes, the tall, sticklike characters of the oldest Germanic alphabet. The Vikings considered runes to be magical, and some of their inscriptions on stones clearly possessed occult meaning; one message, on the underside of a grave slab, instructed that the words must never be exposed to the light of day. Other inscriptions were more mundane. This stone, at Skarby in Sweden, is remarkable for the rearing posture of its fantastical feline beast. But, as the translation below the stone indicates, the runic words are simply commemorative: "Kaulfr and Autir, they erected this stone in memory of Tumi, their brother, who owned Gusnava [a village]."

handles from reindeer horn. In the open marketplaces, from temporary stalls or the tents where they camped during the trading season, Franks peddled glass; Germans hawked basalt millstones and two-handled pottery jars filled with oil or wine. Here, too, human commodities captured in places as far apart as Slavic Russia and Celtic Ireland trod the wood-paved streets. During the 950s, an Arab from Spain with the tongue-twisting name of Ibrahim ibn Ahmed at-Tartushi came to buy slaves and found Hedeby distasteful. Decaying animal sacrifices hung on poles outside the thatched houses, the streets were filthy, the stench was terrific, and the noise appalled him. "Never have I heard such hideous singing as that of the people of this town," he wrote. "It is a growl that comes from the throat, like the baying of dogs, only even more like a wild beast than that."

Trading centers like Hedeby helped set in motion a profound change in Scandinavian religious preferences. Saxons and other Christians went north during the ninth century to minister to foreign merchants concentrated in the market towns, and they even built churches there. From these beginnings, Christianity took root and slowly spread, though not always on its merits. The Danes converted late in the tenth century—largely because their king Harald Bluetooth wanted to stay on the good side of the new German emperor Otto I. And when the Norwegians and Swedes followed a half century or more later, the impetus came from kings who saw that this well-ordered religion, with its hierarchy of bishops, could help them consolidate central authority. Even then, many Vikings retained their old fighting zeal and their heathen deities. One Viking maintained that while he believed in Christ he still made vows to Thor to ensure safety on sea voyages.

Viking commerce had other profound effects at home and abroad. For example, it fostered a flourishing internal trade. To and from Hedeby, Birka, and the other market towns the goods flowed on horse-drawn carts and wagons and, across the frozen rivers and lakes of winter, on sledges accompanied by merchants clomping along in boots with iron spikes or skimming along on flat skates carved from the bones of horses or reindeer. And Viking trade breathed life into commerce all over Europe, establishing routes by river and sea that opened new markets and revived old ones. The profitable Viking trade also had an unwanted side

effect. From its beginnings in the Baltic, it attracted pirates. Most of these raiders were themselves Vikings. Indeed, trading and piracy often were indistinguishable pursuits. A merchant bound for the marketplace seldom hesitated to avail himself of the bounty aboard another ship if opportunity presented itself. Toward the end of the eighth century, Viking activity spread from the Baltic to the North Sea, and Norwegian marauders launched their lightning raids on Lindisfarne and other monasteries on the northeast coast of England—"like stinging hornets," as one English scribe evocatively phrased it.

During this same period, the monastery-studded coast of Ireland farther west also beckoned. These monasteries were centers of intellectual enlightenment in an ancient Celtic society of conflicting petty kingdoms that long had remained isolated from outside influences. But now, a local scribe wrote in the Annals of Ulster for 820, "The sea spewed forth floods of foreigners over Erin, so that no haven, no landing-place, no stronghold, no fort, no castle might be found, but it was submerged by waves of Vikings and pirates."

Ireland became so attractive to the Norwegians that, less than two decades later, they stopped returning home after every plunderous visit. They stayed on to establish coastal strongholds at Dublin, Limerick, Cork, and other sites. For the Irish, these strongholds were mixed blessings. From these bases, the Norwegians made forays inland to plunder cattle, slaves, and church valuables. But the towns also evolved into trading centers that opened the isolated areas of the island to the outside world.

The Norwegians could not keep Ireland to themselves for long. In 851, a fleet of their Viking neighbors from Denmark came looking for a profit. So fierce was the resulting internecine warfare that after one battle, a group of Irishmen found the Danish victors nonchalantly cooking their supper in caldrons placed on heaps of the Norwegian dead. For a hundred years thereafter, Irish, Norwegians, and Danes fought one another in a turbulent kaleidoscope of shifting alliances that saw the sons of Erin partially expel and then gradually absorb the Viking intruders.

Danish involvement in Ireland was a sideshow, however. The Danes began pillaging coastal England in 835 and before long were working both sides of the Channel. After 840, the Frankish Empire, which included present-day France, Germany, and the Low Countries, became their favorite target. The death that year of Charlemagne's son Louis resulted in a breakup of the empire into three kingdoms. The rivalry among Louis's three sons then rendered the Franks vulnerable to outside attacks for the first time since the founding of the Carolingian dynasty in 751.

Danish Vikings ranged up and down the Frankish coast in ever-larger flotillas. They destroyed the Saxon port of Hamburg. On no fewer than six different occasions, they pillaged Dorestad, the leading market town of northern Europe. In 845, they ventured more than 100 miles up the river Seine and sacked Paris on Easter Sunday. They then departed, but only after King Charles the Bald paid them 7,000 pounds of silver. Such payoffs soon became standard practice in both France and England, where they were known as Danegeld, or "Danish money." "Buy off the spear aimed at your breast," went the new saying, "if you do not wish to feel its point."

In the 850s, Viking raiders changed their tactics in Europe. Being a Viking no longer was seasonal employment. Instead of going home to tend to their farms during the winter, the Danes established semipermament bases on islands in the mouths of the big rivers of England and France, bases that served as homes and supply posts for attacks on almost any inland community they chose. These bases put them within

Christianity and paganism coexisted in the Viking world, and many converts to the new religion continued to venerate the old deities. The clever Danish artisan who contrived the soapstone mold at left could cater to both religious tastes, providing customers with silver amulets of the Christian cross and of red-bearded Thor's renowned hammer, Mjollnir—objects such as those shown here. The Swedish amulet above, crafted about AD 1000 and depicting a moustached Viking warrior in a typical helmet with nose guard, may have been meant to protect its possessor in battle.

Dublin, nestled at the confluence of the winding Poddle Creek and the Liffey River estuary on the coast of the Irish Sea, was built from scratch in about AD 840 by an invading Norwegian chieftain named Turgeis, who proclaimed himself "king of all foreigners in Erin." A ruthless pagan, he was later seized by Irish natives and drowned in Lough Owel.

Yet the old Viking had wisely selected his site: Situated athwart vital trade routes reaching to the north, east, and south, Dublin by the late tenth century was an international port of the first rank. Here, as viewed from the north, a cargo vessel makes for the busy shore, where other ships lie snugly moored or beached.

Surrounding the town was an embankment topped by a timber palisade. Inside this protective bulwark as many as 10,000 people were crowded into an area of fewer than fifteen acres. Each family apparently owned its own fenced plot and home. At top left is a compound containing the king's residence; the large structure on the lower right was evidently used for public assemblies. Although the purpose of the tear-shaped central area is unknown, it may have been a market.

A FOOTHOLD IN IRELAND

striking distance of practically every community no matter how far inland or upstream. "The number of ships increases, the endless flood of Vikings never ceases to grow bigger," wrote the Frankish scholar Ermentarius. "Everywhere Christ's people are the victims of massacre, burning, and plunder. The Vikings overrun all that lies before them, and none can withstand them. They seize Bordeaux, Prigueux, Limoges, Angoulme, Toulouse. Angers, Tours, and Orléans are made deserts."

During this period, the Danes—occasionally in company with their sometime rivals the Norwegians—forayed farther south. They hit the Atlantic coast of Moorish Spain, though not always with success: Moors under Abd al-Rahman II sank thirty ships and sent the severed heads of 200 Vikings as a message to their allies in Tangier that the Norsemen were not invulnerable. But the setback was minor. During the next decade, Viking fleets sailed through the Straits of Gibraltar—the Pillars of Hercules— and ravaged towns along the North African shore.

In 860, Danes reached the west coast of Italy. They pillaged Pisa and then, moving on, thought they had come upon Rome itself. Bent upon sacking that storied city, the Viking commander came up with a bizarre ruse. He had a message sent ashore alleging that he, the visitors' chieftain, had just died and needed a Christian burial. The townspeople took the pious bait—and regretted it. After being carried in a coffin to a grave site inside the town, the commander leaped from the bier and drove his sword through the officiating bishop. When he discovered that this was not Rome at all but a place called Luna, he ordered the town burned and its menfolk massacred. He spared the lives of the women, who were carted off for the slave markets.

At this time, however, Viking strategy was evolving beyond such hit-and-run strikes. The movement seems to have begun in Denmark, perhaps because of population pressure, perhaps simply because of desires for new lands to rule. In 865, bands of Vikings began landing on the eastern coast of England under the command of fabled chieftains such as Ivar the Boneless. Unlike their predecessors, they intended to conquer, not merely plunder. The England they found was not one country, but a patchwork of small, quarrelsome kingdoms, established in the fifth century when Angles and Jutes from Denmark and Saxons from farther south had conquered much of Britain, overcoming the native Celts and the remnants of Roman Britain.

Grouped in small armies numbering probably no more than several hundred men, the Danish warriors dressed and fought in typical Viking style. They went into battle wearing some kind of protective garb—a mail shirt of interlinked iron rings, if they could afford it, or a homemade, padded leather jerkin with plates of bone sewn inside. They usually carried a small shield of wood, perhaps reinforced with iron-rimmed leather, and sometimes wore a conical helmet of leather or metal. (The familiar two-horned Viking helmet of legend evidently was worn for religious ceremonies rather than as everyday combat gear.) No matter how they dressed, one chronicler wrote, the Vikings looked so "utterly wild and rough" that "they evidence their bloodthirstiness by their very appearance."

A typical battle began with the Vikings and their Anglo-Saxon opponents arrayed in opposing lines. Each side unleashed a shower of missiles—spears, arrows, stones. Then came the aspect of battle the Vikings relished: hand-to-hand combat. Vikings went at their opponents with thrusting spears that were held in the hand rather than thrown and with their other favorite weapons: swords and battle-axes. The two-edged sword was less than a meter long but heavy. Like the broadax, which carried a flared

The Shipwright's Art

Only through their command of the seas could the Vikings have burst from their frozen homelands to explore, trade, and conquer. And only through the consummate skills of their shipwrights were the people of Scandinavia transformed from coastwise sailors to masters of deepwater voyaging. In the eighth century, Scandinavia's shipbuilders wrought changes that brought Viking craft to a peak of perfection. The key breakthrough was the addition of tall masts and broad sails to ships that had previously been powered by oar alone, along with keels stout enough to support the new gear. At the same time, hulls were ingeniously constructed to be strong yet lightweight and shallow of draft. The combination of seaworthiness and shallow draft enabled the Viking ships to negotiate treacherous open water yet nimbly beach on sandy shores and navigate far upstream in the rivers of Europe. On narrow waterways, for tight maneuvering, crews could lower sail and man the oars. So versatile were these craft that, their sailing days over, they often served Viking spiritual needs—on land, as tombs.

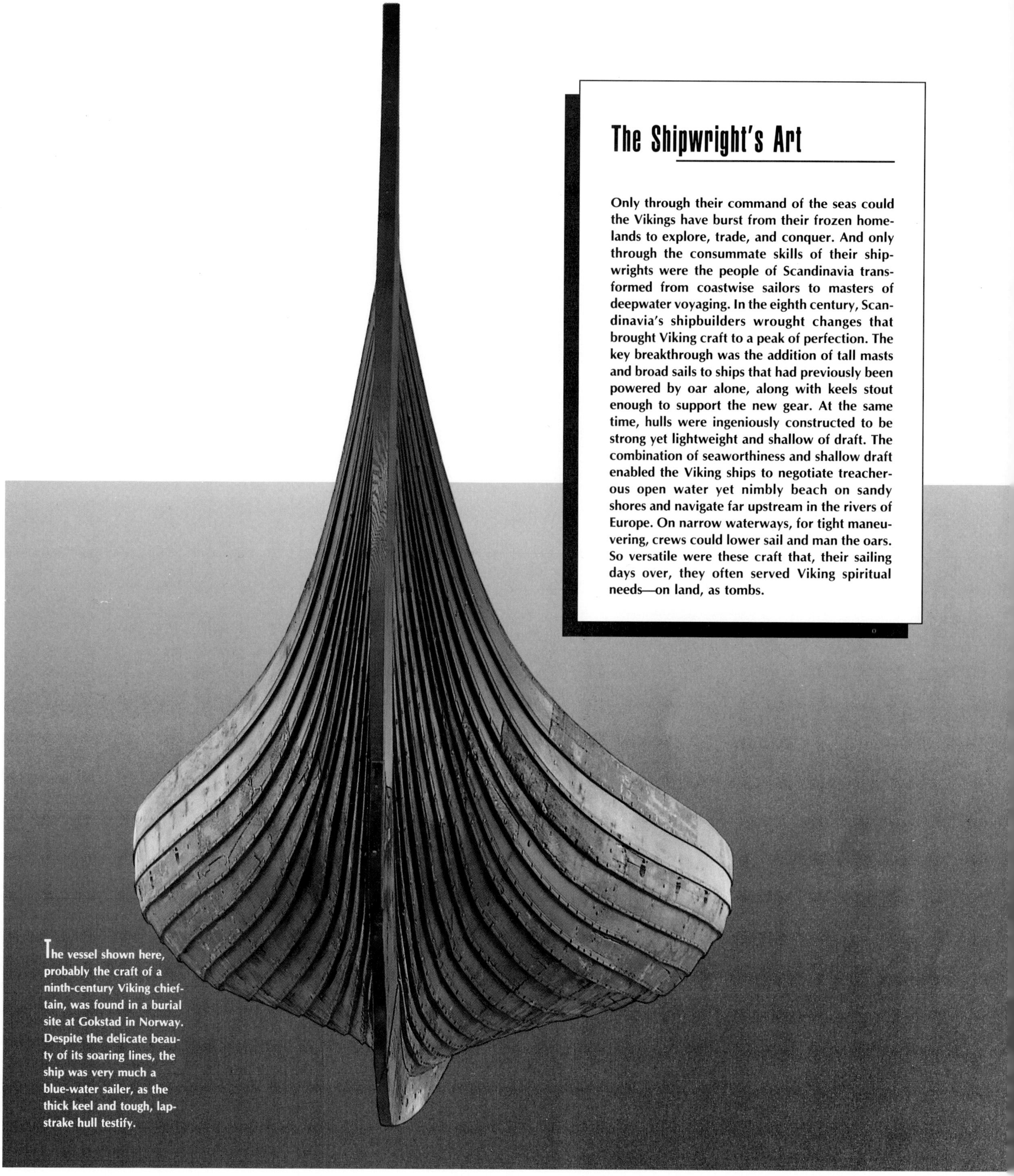

The vessel shown here, probably the craft of a ninth-century Viking chieftain, was found in a burial site at Gokstad in Norway. Despite the delicate beauty of its soaring lines, the ship was very much a blue-water sailer, as the thick keel and tough, lapstrake hull testify.

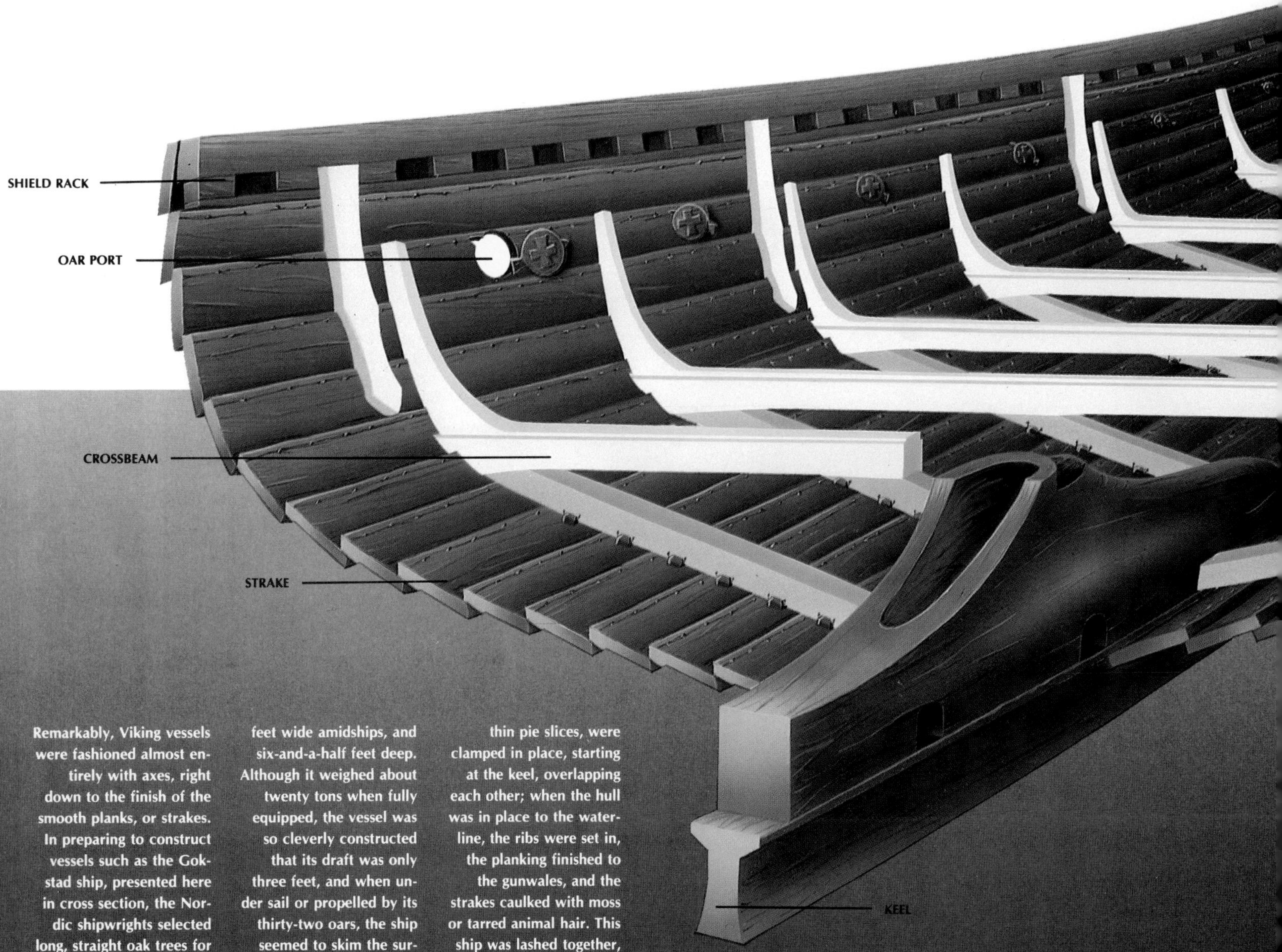

SHIELD RACK —

OAR PORT —

CROSSBEAM —

STRAKE —

KEEL —

Remarkably, Viking vessels were fashioned almost entirely with axes, right down to the finish of the smooth planks, or strakes. In preparing to construct vessels such as the Gokstad ship, presented here in cross section, the Nordic shipwrights selected long, straight oak trees for the keel and the strakes. Crooked trees, as well as forked branches and roots, were used for the vessel's ribs and other curved and irregular parts.

The ship measured seventy-six-and-a-half feet long, seventeen-and-a-half feet wide amidships, and six-and-a-half feet deep. Although it weighed about twenty tons when fully equipped, the vessel was so cleverly constructed that its draft was only three feet, and when under sail or propelled by its thirty-two oars, the ship seemed to skim the surface of the water. Nordic shipwrights built from the outside in. First, the keel was secured to the stem at the bow and the sternpost aft to make a solid spine. Then the strakes, made from logs split radially like extremely thin pie slices, were clamped in place, starting at the keel, overlapping each other; when the hull was in place to the waterline, the ribs were set in, the planking finished to the gunwales, and the strakes caulked with moss or tarred animal hair. This ship was lashed together, rather than nailed as later Viking craft were—a method that gave the craft extraordinary flexibility in heavy seas. Finally, the mast assembly (opposite page) and other equipment were affixed, and the ship was ready to set forth.

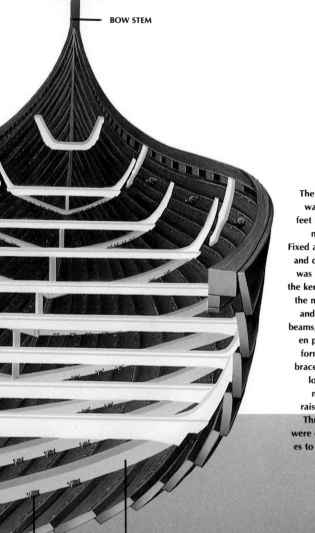

BOW STEM

RIB

LASHING

The Gokstad ship's mast was perhaps thirty-two feet high and weighed as much as 800 pounds. Fixed atop the keel to bear and distribute the burden was a big wooden block, the kerling, with a hole for the mast's foot. Above it, and supported by cross-beams, was a massive oaken piece, called from its form a mast fish, which braced the mast. It had a long slot in which the mast slid while being raised or lowered (top). Three T-shaped trestles were employed as crutches to stow the sail's yard.

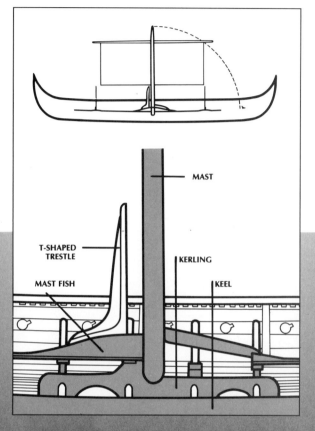

MAST

T-SHAPED
TRESTLE

KERLING

MAST FISH

KEEL

The craft was steered by a rudder made from a single oaken piece eleven feet long and resembling an oar's blade. It was attached to the ship near the stern on the starboard side by a supple willow branch that allowed it to be twisted for steering or rotated out of harm's way when the vessel was beached. To keep the rudder from swinging wildly against the hull in heavy seas, it was secured near the top by a strap.

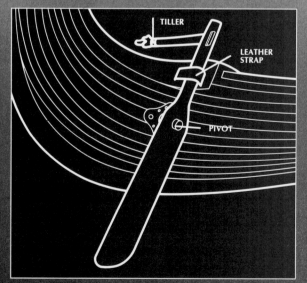

TILLER

LEATHER
STRAP

PIVOT

Despite a penchant for pure ornamentation such as the dragonhead prow with a curling stern-tail, Viking mariners were proudest of their woolen sails: One chieftain loitered a fortnight for a wind that would enable him to parade along a foreign coast with his single sail set at its most attractive angle. However, the diamond pattern on this warship's sail was for a practical reason: The stitched strips reinforced the fabric, preventing it from stretching or shrinking during constant wetting and drying.

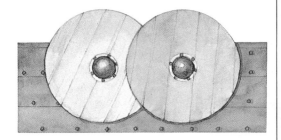

Although warriors' shields were sometimes hung from gunwale racks stem to stern, such a practice was probably ceremonial. On a vessel underway and rolling in the seas, the shields would have been washed away; in calm airs that required rowing the oar ports would have been covered.

THE NIMBLE LONGSHIP

The lightning raids of the Northmen were made possible by the speed and maneuverabilty of their longships. These assets were imparted by the low, slim lines of the warship depicted here in plan views. Although nearly ninety-two feet long, the vessel was only fifteen feet wide and of extremely shallow draft. The shipwrights made every effort to save weight by paring down structural members, and under oar power, the ship was nimble in tight waters and very swift.

Described by one chronicler as a "goat of the sea" for its ability to butt its way for long distances in high seas, the Norse cargo ship was built strictly for business, without frills or comforts. The ship was relatively heavy, particularly when laden, and its crew of perhaps a dozen men depended almost entirely on the sail to make headway, probably using the oars only for maneuvering in harbor. Nearly all the space on board was given over to cargo. Short lengths of decking fore and aft afforded the crewmen with some protection from the elements.

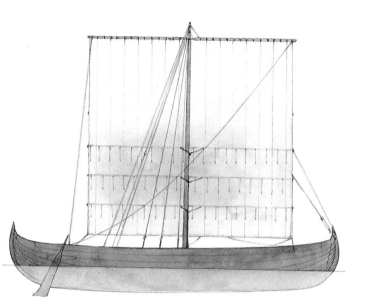

THE CAPRICIOUS KNORR

Broader, blunter, and deeper than the blade-thin longships, merchant vessels made up in carrying capacity and durability what they lacked in style and speed. This trader, or knorr, was about fifty-four feet long and nearly sixteen feet wide, giving it a capacious length-to-width ratio of less than four to one. From keel to gunwale it was more than six feet deep, and there was space in its hold for 1,200 cubic feet of cargo. The internal bracing helped it survive heavy buffeting.

Evidence of the Norse fondness for combining the beautiful and the useful, superbly gilded wind vanes such as the one shown here swung on the prows of longships. On this eleventh-century vane from Norway, a mythical beast stalks a smaller but identical creature, while a sculpted lion, its eyes on the horizon, stands on the tip of the vane. So that it could rotate, the vane *(right)* hung from a metal rod attached to the ship's prow. The holes along the curved edge were for streamers—and the large dents were left there by flying arrows.

head up to twelve inches across and had to be hefted with both hands, it was wielded in a deadly hacking motion. Opposing warriors bashed away until one or the other fell or gave up. Dying bravely brought honor to the Viking warrior, for most believed that his soul would be transported to Valhalla, the great hall of the war god Odin.

One extraordinary group of warriors was particularly devoted to Odin. They fought like men possessed. They rolled their eyes, bit their shields, howled like enraged animals, and sometimes rushed into battle without protective armor—or any clothing at all. These were the berserkir, men whose name derived either from the Old Norse for "bear shirt," meaning that they fought wearing skins, or "bare skin" meaning that they fought unprotected. Their frenzy may have been induced by methods of self-hypnosis such as rhythmic howling and leaping or simply by consuming ale or wine. From them came the Anglicized word "berserk," which symbolized to their English victims the behavior of many of the Viking warriors.

Berserk or merely fighting with Viking ferocity, the Danish invaders found the half dozen small kingdoms of England highly vulnerable. The Danes quickly seized one such kingdom, East Anglia. The following year, 866, they marched northward to the Northumbrian realm and conquered York. When they met opposition, as they did from Northumbrian kings, their response was savage. In 867, for instance, they captured King Ella of Northumbria and subjected him to wanton cruelty: the so-called blood-eagle sacrifice, an unspeakable practice in which the lungs were ripped out of the living victim and the two lobes left to flap like wings with his final dying breaths.

Kingdom after kingdom fell to the merciless Danes. By 880, they controlled much of northern and eastern England. A single kingdom remained in the hands of the Anglo-Saxons, Wessex in the southwestern part of the island, and it stoutly resisted the Vikings. The ruler of Wessex, King Alfred, was Europe's most distinguished sovereign since Charlemagne, and the only English ruler ever to be accorded the epithet "the Great." Like the Frankish emperor, he was at once a scholar who spurred a revival of learning in his realm and an ardent student of statesmanship and warfare.

The statesman in Alfred led him to conclude a peace treaty in 886 with the Danish leader Guthrum. The treaty gave a legal basis to Viking conquests, recognizing Danish hegemony over more than half of England, an area comprising some 25,000 square miles that later came to be known as the Danelaw. But the strategist in Alfred induced him to prepare for renewed warfare. He reformed his army to reduce desertions: Soldiers were rotated from battle areas so that half would always be at home on their farms with their families and half would always be ready for combat. He built a series of fortifications and strongpoints where his people could take refuge during Viking incursions. And he constructed a navy of enormous ships "almost twice as long" as those of the Vikings, according to Anglo-Saxon records.

Alfred's military savvy paid off after war resumed in 892. He anticipated modern military tactics by destroying all the grain and cattle in one region and thus denying it to the enemy. He forced Danes out of their camp twenty miles north of London by building forts on the river Lea and by blocking the river, denying them water. And in 896, he achieved the rare distinction of winning a naval battle against the Vikings. By the time of Alfred's death in 899, the enemy had abandoned their attempts to annex Wessex and settled down in the vast confines of their Danelaw. There, Dane and native Anglo-Saxons lived side by side and got along reasonably well.

The Danish settlers intermarried with the Anglo-Saxons and influenced other aspects of English life. The Scandinavian concepts of trial by jury and majority rule

In this re-creation of a Viking burial, a longship is ready to convey the soul of a young noblewoman from Oseburg, Norway, to the netherworld. On the deck, in a tent-shaped log burial are sacrificial animals that will serve the dead in the otherworld—dogs, horses, and oxen, some of them beheaded. Among the animals are pieces of equipment, including chests for personal

chamber, the body of the woman lies on bedding near that of her attendant. Nearby are essentials for the journey, including a bucket of apples. Strewn about the deck or beside the ship belongings, utensils, carved sleighs, and a decorated cart. Oars at the ready, prow pointing seaward, the ship was buried in a blue-clay trench, covered with rocks, and sealed with sod.

became embedded in Anglo-Saxon law. Scores of new place names, such as Whitby and Grimsby, reflected the addition of the suffix "by," which in old Norse meant farm or village. And the basic similarity between that language and the local dialects resulted in the adoption of thousands of loan words from Old Norse, along with changes in pronunciation, grammar, and syntax. The speaker of modern English cannot utter such basic words as "happy" or "angry" or "ill" or "die" without owing a debt to the Danelaw.

After Alfred's death, control of the Danelaw vacillated between Vikings and English. In 954, the last of the Danish kings of York, Eric Bloodaxe, was deposed, and Northumbria became part of the united kingdom of England. By the end of that century, however, Danish raids on England had been renewed in fleets numbering nearly 100 ships despite huge payments of Danegeld that in the space of two decades amounted to more than 100,000 pounds of silver. Then, in 1017, the famous Dane Canute took over the throne in both England and Denmark.

In France, meanwhile, Danish Vikings also attempted to carve out a realm of their own. Toward the end of the ninth century, they began crossing the channel from bases in newly conquered Danelaw to mount river assaults on inland Frankish cities. But the resistance around these cities stiffened. For example, at Paris, on the upper reaches of the Seine, the Franks built fortified bridges to block the river. These efforts proved effective: In 886, a Danish armada was forced to abandon the assault on Paris after a siege of nearly a year. By concentrating on this inland region, however, the Franks left the coastal reaches of the Seine at the mercy of the Vikings.

In 911, the king of the western Franks hit upon a novel solution to this problem. King Charles decided to cede the area surrounding the mouth of the Seine to the Vikings, who controlled most of it anyway. In return for the land and the title Count of Rouen, their chieftain, Rollo, swore fealty to Charles and agreed to help protect the Seine valley against rival Vikings. Rollo's men soon came to be called Normans—a contraction of Northmen—and their duchy in northwestern France, which they quickly expanded at the expense of their new neighbors, was known as Normandy.

Rollo kept his bargain with King Charles. He even agreed to give up his heathen religion and be baptized a Christian. His Vikings melded into the local culture much more rapidly than in England. They took local women as wives and concubines and watched their children grow up speaking the Frankish tongue. Virtually all traces of their old ways—from Scandinavia and from the Danelaw of England—vanished. Later, however, in one of history's ironic twists, their descendants would return to England in 1066 under the command of Rollo's sixth-generation descendant William the Conqueror and put an end to that kingdom's turbulent Viking era.

While the Danes settled in already-populated regions of England and France, the Norwegians set about colonizing lands that were essentially virgin. Even in the raiding days of the ninth century, bands of Norwegians settled in parts of Britain to farm. Colonies took root in Scotland and on its islands—the Orkneys, Hebrides, and Isle of Man. Viking settlers also ventured north onto the Shetland Islands and then west to the Faroes, about 425 miles from Norway.

And the Faroes became stepping-stones to the large island 280 miles farther west in the North Atlantic: Iceland. Vikings discovered Iceland by accident in about 860, when two separate ships were blown off course on voyages from Scandinavia to the Faroes and Hebrides. Although one member of a landing party unaccountably reported that every blade of grass dripped with butter, this did not seem at first sight a promising location for colonization. The large island was blanketed by ice caps, lava beds, volcanic mountains, and rock-littered moraines. Only about one-sixth of its 40,000 square miles was fit for human habitation.

Such was the Norse demand for land, however, that within a decade, settlement began in force. The majority of settlers came from southwestern Norway, looking for a new farm or fleeing the forced consolidation of Norway's petty kingdoms by King Harald Fairhair. They had to endure a 700-mile journey that took them via the Shetlands and the Faroes, often through fierce storms. Such was their sailing skill that they accomplished the crossing in a remarkable five or six days. Other emigrants of Norwegian stock journeyed from Ireland and the islands around Scotland.

These Icelandic pioneers made the most of it. The landscape was harsh, but the climate, warmed by an arm of the Gulf Stream, proved to be moderate enough for the cultivation of grain. Grass good enough for their sheep—though not a single blade dripped with butter—grew in the fertile valleys of the fjords and in the upper moorlands. Tough, homespun woolen cloth soon became the principal export, so prized in this pioneer region where goods were rare, though silver was plentiful, that it was recognized as a standard unit of monetary exchange. The settlers, lacking hardwood forests, framed their houses with driftwood they gathered. Surrounded by soft volcanic stone that was useless for building, they dug up the turf and put together well-insulated walls of sod up to six feet thick.

By 930, Iceland had about 20,000 people and its own unusual system of government and laws. The latter, like the people, came from Norway. But the Icelanders adapted the laws to local circumstances and, while retaining strong trade ties with the home country, fiercely asserted their own political independence. (The Shetland and Orkney Islands, by contrast, became colonies under the Norwegian crown in the eleventh century.) Every summer, Iceland's freemen convened for a fortnight in a national assembly called the Althing. Like the Things of Scandinavia, it tried cases as well as making laws. The Althing was controlled by thirty-six prominent landowners called godar—godly ones—evidently because they originally performed some priestly functions. The freemen pledged allegiance to the chieftains of their home districts, rejecting the idea of a king or other single central authority. The system worked because the island's remoteness obviated the need to unite behind one leader to meet external aggression.

The chieftains elected the lawspeaker, who presided over sessions of the Althing and literally spoke the law. It was his duty to commit to memory all of the laws of the land, which in the absence of a written legal code had to be transmitted orally, and then to recite one-third of them at each annual meeting. These laws ranged from archaic beliefs—for example, the making of a verse in praise of a girl was a serious offense because poetry appeared to have a spellbinding effect—to remarkably progressive legislation for mutual insurance. The latter provided for local communal units, consisting of at least twenty farmers, which partially reimbursed members for livestock lost to disease or for farm buildings and their contents destroyed by fire.

Under its rudimentary form of parliamentary government, Iceland's population prospered and grew. By the 980s, a century or so after colonization began, it numbered more than 60,000 inhabitants—nearly one-fourth of Norway's population. All the good land was taken, and ambitious Icelanders eager for a new start again looked westward through the mists of the North Atlantic—this time to Greenland.

The catalyst in this newest Norse colonization was an archetypal Viking named Eirik the Red. Literally an outlaw, Eirik, then in his thirties, had red hair, a red beard, and a messy background of involvement in lethal blood feuds. He had been outlawed from Norway along with his father for killing enemies of the family. In Iceland, he twice figured in murderous feuds with neighbors, and on the second occasion, in 982, the local Thing banished him from the island for three years.

Eirik made good use of the time. He and a band of adventurers sailed off in search of the large island a Viking had reported spotting a half century or so before. They found it some 450 miles west of Iceland, sailed around the ice cliffs on its eastern coast, and marked out a settlement on the grass-bordered fjords of the southwest at a suitable distance from the island's ice cap. At the end of his banishment, Eirik returned home to gather colonists for this ice-bound place that, in a moment of unbridled imagination, he had dubbed Greenland. "Men will be more readily persuaded to go there, if the land has an attractive name," he explained.

He was persuasive. In the summer of 986, Eirik sailed again for Greenland at the head of twenty-five ships, each laden with up to forty men, women, and children, along with their livestock. Only fourteen ships carrying about 450 people arrived safely; the others turned back or went down in storms among the mammoth ice floes drifting southward from the polar pack. Under the leadership of Eirik, the erstwhile outlaw, the pioneers farmed, hunted whale and walrus, developed trade with Norway, and established an independent society based on the Icelandic pattern.

Eirik's colonization of Greenland led to one last great Viking achievement—a reaching out to the very shores of America nearly five centuries before Christopher Columbus. In that summer of 986, when Eirik led his party of settlers to Greenland, a young shipmaster, Bjarni Herjolfsson, returned to Iceland from Norway with a consignment of cargo for his father only to find he already had departed with Eirik's fleet. Determined to follow, Bjarni sailed west, got lost, and came upon a land with low hills covered by woods but no glaciers. The lack of ice and mountains told Bjarni this was not his destination. He sailed back toward the northeast and found Greenland without having set foot on the shore of the New World he had glimpsed.

Fifteen years later, Eirik's son Leif did land. In 1001, relying on Bjarni's advice and ship, which he bought, Leif Eirikson followed his route in reverse making landings at Baffin Island, Labrador, and the northern tip of Newfoundland, where in an area today named L'Anse aux Meadows, he and his crew of thirty-five apparently built houses and spent the winter before returning home.

Leif called the place Vinland because of the grapevines he said he found there. No grapes could have grown that far north, of course, but other wild berries such as gooseberries and cranberries, which might have been used for winemaking, were abundant. Or it may be that Leif, as his father had done, was merely gilding his account to attract settlers. In 1009, an expedition of 250 men and women under Thorfinn Karlsefni, an Icelander who had married the widow of Leif's brother, established a settlement farther south in Vinland. After nearly three years, troubles with the local people—either Eskimo or Algonquin Indians—forced them to return to Greenland. But houses, possibly built by Leif, remained at L'Anse aux Meadows. If they are Viking remains, they provide mute testimony of that remarkable era when the Northmen—pirates and traders, explorers and settlers—bestrode both worlds, the old and the new, from the banks of the Russian Volga to the shores of the American Vinland, as none had done before and few thereafter.

A LUST FOR PRECIOUS METALS

Wherever they lived and wherever they went, they left a trail of buried treasure. More than 1,000 caches of silver objects, and some of gold, would later be unearthed in their Norse homelands, and countless others were left underground across the vast expanse through which they roamed, from the Ural Mountains in the east to Iceland in the west.

Some of the hoards were small, containing only a handful of coins or a couple of ornaments. But a number of hidden collections contained as much as eighteen pounds of precious artifacts, while the biggest of them all, a huge assortment buried at Cuerdale in northwestern England, weighed nearly ninety pounds. Whatever the size of the treasure or wherever it was stashed, hidden wealth represented all that was dearest to the Viking heart—and in riches like the gilded sword and scabbard pictured here, the Vikings left a shining legacy of their age.

Erupting from the darkened closet of their native north, where no precious metals were mined, the Vikings nurtured an understandable lust for that which gleamed and glittered in the sun's rays. Yet by no means was the obsession merely aesthetic: For the Nordic warrior, the plunder he took was the measure of his success in life. Silver, showily displayed in ornamental ways, was thus a status symbol in Scandanavian society and a potent inducement that attracted followers and helped build personal armies for the warfare that was a constant theme of Viking life.

But silver was also the currency of the realm, and whenever the Vikings were torn between their love of beautiful jewelry and their need for ready capital for trading or other enterprises, the practical requirements invariably prevailed. One Icelandic saga, for example, tells of how fellow citizens decided to reward a famed poet named Eyvind Skaldaspillir for his work. Silver coins "of full weight" were collected by public subscription, then melted and shaped into a handsome shoulder pin for Eyvind—who promptly broke it into bits and used the pieces to purchase a farm for himself. Such was the common metamorphosis of Viking silver, cycled and recycled from coins to adornments and from adorn-

ments to currency of various sorts—until, in many cases, it was eventually hidden in the Northern earth or in the bogs of some faraway land.

Such caches would tell future generations much of the story of the Viking age. During most of the ninth and tenth centuries, when Nordic traders thrust deep into Russia and met with Arab merchants, an overwhelming preponderance of the wealth that later found its way into hoards was in the coinage of the caliphate. By the 970s, however, strife in the Volga region apparently interrupted trade, and at any rate the great Islamic silver mines were then beginning to peter out. By about that time, Germany's Harz Mountain deposits had become the major source of silver for western Europe, with results that later appeared in hidden Viking treasures. Moreover, it was perhaps in direct response to the dwindling supply of Muslim silver that the Northmen levied their heavy tax upon England—the Danegeld. Between 991 and 1014, the Danegeld brought them an amount of silver equivalent to 36 million coins, according to one chronicle.

Why did they secrete so much of their wealth in the ground? Some of it, to be sure, was probably buried as offerings to pagan gods. Even more went underground in the belief, as described in one saga, that whatever a warrior placed in the earth would be available to him in Valhalla. Yet beyond question the major reason was also the most obvious—for safekeeping. The Norsemen lived in tumultuous times. It was Viking against Viking and Vikings against the world. And what they hid to protect, they frequently never lived to recover.

The Vikings appraised silver by its weight, not by the face value of coins. In this hoard (left) from Birka in Sweden, some coins were cut in half to equal exact amounts needed for transactions. The arm rings could be worn for adornment or broken into pieces for use in trade. Since gold was scarce, treasures such as the one above, from Norway, were rare. The larger neck ring weighs more than 2½ pounds, but the prize piece is the exquisite trefoil brooch of Frankish origin.

Although Viking artisans at first tended to copy foreign designs in making ornaments, in time they developed their own styles. This eleventh century silver armband, fashioned in a Swedish shop, appears simple in its conception. Yet the patterns of inlaid enamel on the snake's back, while resembling the creature's skin, are in fact representative of plant tendrils and lobes, one of the most popular Viking motifs of the time.

The thick woolen cloak worn by Viking men was sometimes fastened by a brooch with a long, sharp pin—such as the one at left—which was topped by rings in which the heavy material was bunched. The cape was usually pinned at the right shoulder, so that the part allowed its owner freedom to use his sword hand. Because of its dainty design of gilded silver with niello inlays, this pin from Birka was likely used only on festive occasions. The colorful and elaborate necklaces from Sweden (right) would have adorned wealthy Nordic ladies.

If, as it appears, this elegant, drum-shaped brooch were indeed made entirely of gold and silver, it would have been worth a small Viking fortune. Instead, the artist in Gotland who made the piece applied a thin veneer of precious metals to a bronze form. Nearly three inches in diameter, it was created for a noblewoman.

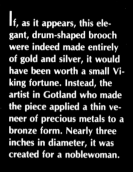

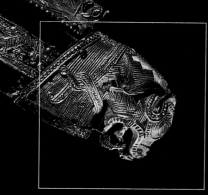

Aristocratic Vikings favored gleaming ornamentation with intricate designs for even the most utilitarian articles. Above, a wooden horse collar with extravagant gilded mountings was used for no higher purpose than as part of the harness for a cart in tenth-century Jutland. The detail at near left is a bestial end piece from the same collar whose creature, with its wild eyes and snarling visage, is typical of the demonic forces that were both feared and admired by the Vikings.

BYZANTIUM RESURGENT

It all began with an unruly horse. The emperor Michael III, lord of what would later be known as the Byzantine Empire, loved horses above most things. Racing the beautiful beasts was the emperor's lifelong passion, infinitely more interesting than tedious affairs of state. Indeed, to Michael III, governing his troubled domain, which by the year AD 858 had been reduced to a fraction of the colossal empire bequeathed by Justinian three centuries before, was an irksome business much better sloughed off onto the shoulders of other people.

But the unmanageable horse, so spirited that no one could ride or drive it, was quite another matter. When attempt after attempt to control the animal ended in curses and failure, the emperor sank into a black depression, accentuated by heavy drink. This was a condition of mortal peril to all those around him, for Michael was capable of great cruelty, and even sudden executions, whenever frustrated or provoked.

At considerable risk to himself, therefore, one of the emperor's entourage stepped forward. He had in his employ a groom, he told the emperor, a remarkably strong and gifted peasant from Macedonia named Basil, who might be able to handle the animal. Basil was summoned. He proved to be a young man of twenty-two, a magnificent physical specimen gifted with great presence. Under Michael's doleful gaze, Basil stepped toward the horse.

The confrontation between man and beast was marvelous to behold. With one immensely powerful hand, Basil grasped the bridle of the plunging horse and by main force, compelled the stallion to stand still. Next, with his other hand, he reached up, gripped the quivering animal's ear, and spoke into it in low tones. It took but a moment, and then, as if by some celestial command, the untamable horse was transformed into a docile servant of the emperor.

Michael the Drunkard—as he would be known, so descriptively, to posterity—was instantly transported from the deepest despair to euphoria. Whooping with joy, he decided to draft Basil into his personal service, as a member of the imperial palace guard. And by this simple, solitary act, Michael unwittingly set in motion a series of events that ultimately would lead to some of the greatest achievements of the Byzantine Empire, to the establishment of the second-longest-lived dynasty in its thousand-year history—and to his own assassination.

Less than a decade after Basil's astonishing feat of horsebreaking, the unlettered peasant from the far provinces would step across the dead body of his mentor to assume the imperial throne and launch the second golden age of Byzantium. For nearly two centuries thereafter, while the lights of civilization flickered low in western Europe, the glory of the Byzantines would continue to blaze with a dazzling luminosity from the East.

There, a remarkable amalgam of peoples—called Greeks by western Europeans,

Romans by Middle Eastern Arabs, but simply Christians by themselves—harnessed to their benefit a disparate but powerful set of forces and values: the efficient military and civil authority that was the legacy of the old Roman Empire; the rich cultural heritage of classical Greece; the vigorous spirituality of the Christian church; and the enormous wealth endowed by the empire's strategic position astride the bustling trade routes between Asia and Europe.

A number of drawbacks accompanied these considerable advantages. The great legions and the enormous bureaucracy required to administer the provinces were not only hugely expensive, but a breeding ground of corruption and connivance. The Church, for all its vitality and high purpose, was wracked by disputes between the pope in Rome and the patriarch in Constantinople. Moreover, it was torn by frequent, tumultuous battles between theological factions, each of which claimed exclusive possession of the truth and considered all opponents to be heretics. As for the wealth that infused the empire, it was a magnet for less-fortunate, but ever-ambitious, enemies eager to improve their lot through war and conquest.

Despite these problems, the Byzantine Empire persevered—now driven into retreat, now expanding throughout the known world; now riven by bloody strife, now forged anew in rediscovered unity. In so doing, the Byzantines preserved some of the highest achievements of human society, most particularly Greek culture, that elsewhere had been trampled into the dust to await a later renaissance. Yet the Byzantines accomplished much more than perseverance and preservation. For all their conservatism—love of

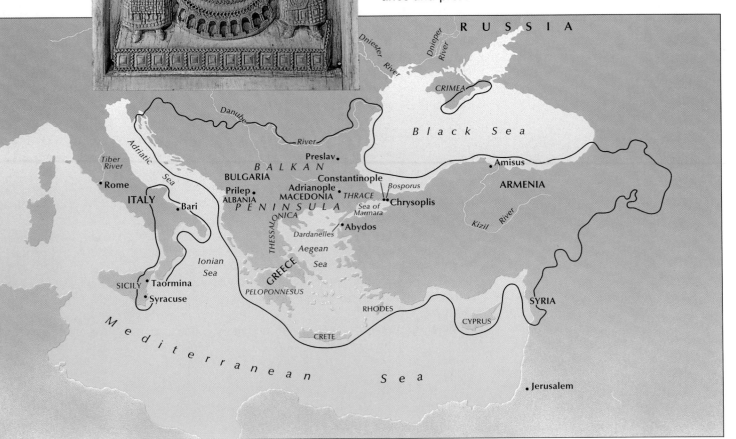

ritual and a profound dislike for change were hallmarks of their era just as much as the passion for labyrinthine intrigue for which their leaders would be remembered—the eastern heirs of Rome slowly transformed themselves. They achieved a remarkable fusion of East and West, of old and new, of pragmatism and mysticism, whose like had not been seen before.

Even before his golden opportunity with the emperor, the man who would be renowned as Basil the Macedonian had experienced more than a little good luck. His origins were rude: He had been born in 836 to a poverty-stricken couple eking out an existence on a small tract of land near Adrianople, and as a restless youth, he had fled the provinces to find his fortune in Constantinople. There was at the time no more glittering city in the entire world. The Byzantine capital had just celebrated its 500th birthday, having been inaugurated by the emperor Constantine in 330 as his new imperial seat. Until then, the settlement located along the waterway that divided Europe from Asia had been known as Byzantium, in commemoration of its founder, a Greek colonizer named Byzas. But after it became the capital, everyone referred to it as the City of Constantine—Constantinople.

It would have been an overwhelming sight to a peasant lad passing through the monumental gates for the first time. Constantinople teemed with a quarter of a million people: slaves and merchants, farmers and diplomats, soldiers and philosophers, everyone jostling through the maze of narrow residential streets and thronging the broad ceremonial avenues.

There was no special section of the city set aside for the wealthy and aristocratic. Palaces and tenements, fine homes and hovels were all jumbled together in one stupendous metropolis. The residences of the rich were built on the Roman model, presenting blank walls to the street and facing inward around courtyards graced with gardens and fountains. More modest houses were built with balconies or windows overlooking the streets so that people could keep track of neighborhood doings in their idle moments. City authorities tried to impose at least a little order to the buildings: All balconies had to be at least fifteen feet off the ground and could not extend to within ten feet of the opposite wall. There were strict regulations about drainage and health, as well: All drains had to lead to the sea, and no one, with the exception of a royal personage, could be buried within the city proper. Each district had its medical officers.

Here and there, the streets opened onto magnificent public gardens and plazas, which were called forums. At almost every corner, it seemed, was a church, sometimes with attached monasteries, hospitals, and orphanages. Through the forums ran great avenues lined with arcades and shops, the various trades and crafts being arranged conveniently in related groups—silversmiths were placed in the vicinity of goldsmiths, purveyors of silks and other textiles were all located in one area, woodworkers and furniture dealers were in another.

The most important of the avenues was the Mese, the triumphal route used for imperial parades. It led in a grand, two-mile sweep from the Golden Gate on the fortified, landward side of the city eastward to the Augustaeum, the main public square, located near the tip of the peninsula jutting between the Sea of Marmara and the Bosporus. Adjoining this square were the principal buildings of the empire, structures of supreme splendor. Here was the Sacred Imperial Palace, residence of the emperor—a seemingly endless series of apartments, throne rooms, gardens, and

Even as the Vikings were raiding Christian sanctuaries along the Atlantic, the rulers of the Byzantine Empire—who saw themselves as Christ's appointed representatives *(inset)*—were facing stiff challenges from Muslim forces in the Mediterranean and from assorted foes in Europe, notably the Bulgars. In 867, Basil I took the throne and launched an era of fitful expansion. In subsequent reigns the crown suffered periodic reversals, as enemy troops surged more than once to the gates of Constantinople, and palace intrigue brought several emperors to bitter ends. Finally, in 976, the ruthless Basil II came to power and proceeded to crush his opponents at home and abroad. In the wake of his long reign, the Byzantine Empire embraced all the land outlined at left—more than it would ever claim again.

chapels wherein the eye was constantly drawn to the gleam of gold and the glitter of precious gems. Nearby stood the Church of Hagia Sophia, or Holy Wisdom, its vast interior spaces aglow with the sheen of varied, carefully fitted marbles bathed with light from the windows girdling the enormous central dome. Here, too, was found the Hippodrome, the city's enormous arena, where 60,000 spectators could watch exciting chariot races, solemn religious processions, official state ceremonies, or grim public executions.

From the windows and the hilltops, one could look north across the city's harbor, the Golden Horn, with its wharves and warehouses and ceaseless bustle of craft bringing silk, aloes, cloves, and sandalwood from Indochina, pepper from Malabar, copper from India, gems from Ceylon—all to be exchanged for amber, furs, metals, and slaves from the north and, of course, for imperial coinage; the currency of Byzantium was the preferred medium everywhere.

In this vast city's roiling sea of humanity, the young peasant Basil exhibited an uncommon buoyancy from the day he arrived from Macedonia. His good luck manifested itself almost at once, as soon as he made his way through the Golden Gate and, with night falling, sought shelter among the usual crowd of destitute in the nearby Church of St. Diomedes. That very evening, he met and gained the favor of the monk in charge. One story said that the monk, Nicholas, was awakened in the night by a strange voice that commanded: "Arise and bring the Basileus into the sanctuary." Nicholas left his pallet and went into the church, but saw nothing except a man asleep in the vestibule. He returned to his slumbers and was awakened a second time by the same voice, with the same result. The third time, the monk felt himself prodded in the side by a sword, and the voice impatiently commanded: "Go out and bring in the man you see lying outside the gate." Nicholas hastened to obey—and in the morning, he took Basil to a bathhouse, gave him fresh clothing, and adopted him as a brother. Or such was the story.

What is certain is that the monk befriended Basil and through his brother, a court physician, secured for the peasant lad a position as a groom in the employ of a rich nobleman. It was impossible not to be impressed with the youth's physical prowess, hunting ability, and engaging personality. Basil quickly became a favorite of his employer, and when the courtier was sent on a mission to the Peloponnesus, he took his young groom with him. On that journey, fortune once again smiled broadly on the Macedonian peasant.

There, in the Peloponnesus, Basil caught the eye of a fabulously wealthy widow named Danielis. She was so impressed with Basil that she lavished on him gold, slaves, and a wardrobe, the sole condition being that he become a "spiritual brother" to her son. Shortly after, the remarkable Macedonian performed his magic on the emperor's horse and entered the imperial household.

Thus far Basil had risen in station largely on the basis of his physical abilities. Now he found himself enmeshed in the plots and jealousies that flared continually among the members of the emperor's court, and he proved as adept at turning these complex machinations to his own ends as he had been at managing horses. Moreover, his luck remained with him. A bitter antagonism developed between the imperial high chamberlain and the emperor Michael's uncle Bardas, the caesar. It was an unequal contest, and the outcome was virtually predetermined. Not only were blood relations involved, but the position of caesar made Bardas the designated successor to the imperial throne. Outweighed on all fronts, the chamberlain eventually lost his post and, more tragically, his freedom. His replacement was none other than Basil.

Ever the willing aide, Basil cemented his position when the emperor decided on a revision of his and the Macedonian's domestic arrangements. Both were already married, Basil to a woman from his homeland and Michael to an empress chosen for him by his mother when he was seventeen years old. But Michael had long preferred the company of his mistress, Eudocia Ingerina. Now, perhaps to give her presence at court a belated legitimacy, Michael directed that Basil divorce his wife and marry Eudocia. Then, to compensate for the loss of Basil's wife and the fact that Eudocia would continue to sleep with the emperor, Michael arranged for his sister Thecla to become Basil's mistress.

While Michael was thus preoccupied with bedrooms, carousing, and horseracing, numerous problems were assailing his empire, which—unlike the earlier Western Roman Empire under such dissolute emperors as Nero and Caligula—was being managed with great capability. This was due entirely to the firm hand and shrewd judgment of Michael's uncle Bardas, the caesar.

Bardas had come to power in 856, just two years before Basil's appearance at court. His ascent had been a masterpiece of manipulation. Understanding full well that Michael, still in his teens, was impatient to be rid of his nagging mother and two regents, Bardas had conspired with the youth to seize control of the throne. The plot concluded with the murder of the principal regent and the banishment of the dowager empress to a convent. Michael turned unfettered to his debauchery, only too happy to leave the vexing business of government to Bardas.

Despite all his ruthlessness, Bardas proved to be a surprisingly dedicated and incorruptible administrator. The decade following his rise to power was a period gilded with significant accomplishments. He founded a great university at the Magnaura Palace in Constantinople and gathered there the most prominent thinkers of the age. And under his guidance, the word of Christ and the power of Byzantium were vigorously exported to heathen lands.

In 864, two brothers, Constantine and Methodius of Thessalonica, conducted a brilliant mission in the north that led to the conversion of the Slavs of Moravia, a land that eventually would be part of Czechoslovakia. In order to explain his Christian religion and celebrate its rituals, Constantine thought to translate the scriptures and the liturgy into the local tongue. But the Moravians had no written language of their own; in response, Constantine—who later became a monk and was canonized as Saint Cyril—invented for them the script that, in modified form, would become the widely used Cyrillic alphabet.

However, conversion of the Moravian Slavs, who had for centuries been exposed to Byzantine civilization, was one thing; more impressive was the success of Bardas's regime in dealing with the fierce Bulgars, who had conquered the Slavic tribes in the Balkans north of Greece. The Bulgars had recently relinquished their nomadic ways, learned to farm, and adopted the language and much of the culture of the Slavs. Yet they remained stubbornly pagan in their religion and aloof in other ways from the empire to the south.

All this began to change in the middle of the ninth century when both the Western, Frankish Empire and the Byzantines started campaigning in earnest for the friendship of the increasingly powerful Bulgars under their khan Boris I. At first Boris saw his best advantage in an alliance with the West and was on the point of making it official when the alarmed Byzantines acted. The imperial army suddenly materialized, mas-

VYING FOR DIVINE FAVOR

The Byzantine emperors were not the only Christian rulers of the day to claim a mandate from heaven. The Frankish king Charlemagne assumed that distinction in the year 800 when Pope Leo III crowned him Emperor of the West at Saint Peter's in Rome—an act regarded in Constantinople as a deliberate affront. Curiously, this ruler who vied with the Byzantines for God's favor was at his death laid in a pagan sarcophagus *(right)* showing the Greek heroine Persephone being separated from her mother, Ceres, goddess of vegetation, and hustled off to the underworld by Hades in a four-horse chariot. The scene may have appealed to Charlemagne as a parable of resurrection, for Persephone was said to return from the dead each spring to renew the earth. Such pagan associations were deemed by later rulers to be inappropriate for the founder of a sacred empire. In the twelfth century, following Charlemagne's canonization, the Holy Roman Emperor Frederick I commissioned a new resting place *(below)* for the saint. At one end of this shrine *(far right)* sat Charlemagne, with Pope Leo III to his right, Bishop Turpin of Rheims to his left—and Christ above, sanctioning the king's rule just as he did in the imperial portraits of Byzantium.

Built in the shape of a church, this oak wood shrine overlaid with gold, silver, and precious stones was dedicated at Aachen in 1215 as Charlemagne's new casket. Scenes from his life adorn the roof; his successors are presented in the alcoves below.

Carved in Italy in the second century, this marble sarcophagus was carried to Charlemagne's court in Aachen to hold the king's remains. Persephone appears at center, in the grasp of Hades, while at far left Ceres mounts a chariot pulled by dragons in an unsuccessful effort to retrieve her daughter.

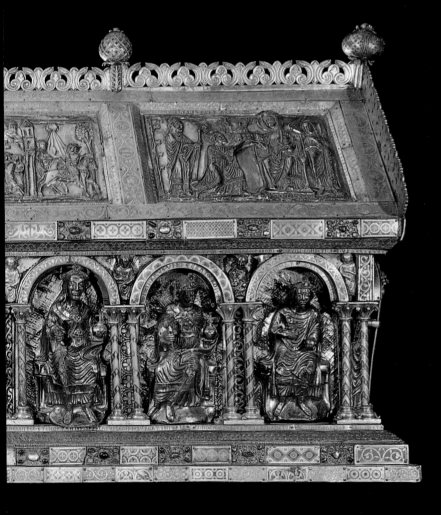

sive and menacing, on the Bulgarian border, and the imperial navy hovered offshore in the Black Sea. Thus reminded of the might and proximity of the Byzantines, Boris underwent a sudden change of heart. In September of 865, he and a number of his most prominent noblemen submitted to baptism by a bishop sent to the Bulgars from Constantinople. In the custom of the day, that act was a statement of Boris's acceptance of both the spiritual values of Christianity and the secular authority of the Byzantine emperor, Christ's regent on earth—a submission to alien powers that was not likely to be acceptable to all of the Bulgars.

The reaction was not long in coming. Some of the old Bulgar clans rose in fury and launched a bloody revolt, the aim of which was to slay Boris and restore paganism. The rebels very nearly succeeded. But after rallying his faithful supporters, Boris won a narrow—some said miraculous—victory and then took his total revenge. On his orders, the rebel leaders, fifty-two in number, were brutally slaughtered, along with all of their children. Boris then settled down to practice Christianity and enjoy the fruits of his new position as the Byzantine emperor's spiritual son and his nation's enviable membership in the Byzantine commonwealth. Among the greatest of the benefits were the vast and profitable trade arrangements now made possible across much of the known world.

Bardas was similarly successful almost everywhere. Byzantine fortunes were clouded only by a deepening split with the Western church in Rome, by the incessant battles with Arab raiders from the south, and by a new threat that had appeared with stunning abruptness in 860. One June afternoon that year, when Bardas, accompanied by Michael, was campaigning against the Arabs, a great fleet of 200 longships sailed into the Sea of Marmara. These were Vikings who had conquered the Slavic tribes of northwestern Asia and had settled in the regions around Kiev. Although they were known as Varangians, they referred to themselves as Rus and eventually would be known as Russians.

Unhurriedly, the Varangians laid waste to the cities of Thrace and then besieged Constantinople itself. The imperial army was recalled, but there was no hope of its arriving in time. "Woe is me," lamented the patriarch Photius to his frightened congregation in Hagia Sophia, "that I see a fierce and savage tribe fearlessly poured round the city, ravaging the suburbs, destroying everything, ruining everything, fields, houses, herds, beasts of burden, women, children, old men, youths, thrusting their swords through everything, taking pity on nothing, sparing nothing."

Photius's chief defensive move was to take from its sanctuary one of the most sacred relics of the Eastern church—a robe believed to have been worn by the Virgin Mary—and parade it in fervent procession around the walls of the city. It was an act that indicated the depth of Byzantine religious conviction; like previous and similar shows of faith, it seemed to protect the city. Shortly after the procession, the raiders lifted the siege and departed as swiftly as they had come. Photius found his reputation greatly enhanced, and the homeward-rushing army returned to its successful campaign against the Arabs. Nevertheless, this first Russian attack on Constantinople deeply alarmed the Byzantines, and they immediately sought alliances with various Slavic peoples against the Varangians.

Internal concerns, also, were very much on Bardas's mind at this time. Chief among them was Michael's increasing enchantment with Basil, the peasant-become-high-chamberlain. For all his sagacity and success, Bardas was forever subject to the emperor's whim, and he was under no illusions as to his master's long-term stability.

His worst fears, as subsequent events grimly testified, were all too well founded.

In the spring of 866, as he and Michael were preparing to lead an expedition against the Saracens based on Crete, Basil convinced the emperor that Bardas was plotting against the throne. The rest followed as predictably as night does day. At a council of war, as Bardas was reviewing army preparedness, Basil and his henchmen suddenly fell upon the old caesar and hacked him to death in the very presence of the emperor, who had assented to the killing but felt himself endangered by the sudden violence of the attack.

Now Michael had no true ally but Basil, and he clung ever closer to his protégé. Michael notified the patriarch of Constantinople that Bardas had been convicted of treason and executed. He not only gave to Basil the powers that had been exercised by Bardas, but adopted the Macedonian as his son. Even this was not sufficient for Basil's expanding ambition.

During elaborate ceremonies in celebration of Whitsunday in May of 866, in the magnificent Hagia Sophia, Michael astonished his court with a proclamation read by his secretary: "It is my will that Basil, the High Chamberlain, since he is faithful to me and protects my sovereignty and delivered me from my enemy and has much affection for me, should be the guardian and manager of my empire and should be proclaimed by all as emperor." The cunning peasant boy now received an imperial crown and took his place beside Michael as co-emperor.

As Bardas had before him, Basil demonstrated a remarkable aptitude for rule. Like Bardas, too, he could not escape the thought that what the emperor had given with such ease, he could with very little trouble take away: Basil's newly gained power was delegated at Michael's pleasure, not conferred as permanent authority actually equal to that held by the emperor.

And Michael's pleasure was erratic. He sank ever deeper into debauchery. He drank constantly, spent wildly, and became increasingly cruel. In drunken rages, which he could not remember the next day, he ordered the execution of innocent men whose only crime was to pass before his maniacal eye. To pay for his excesses, he confiscated church and private property, melting down irreplaceable works of art for their gold content.

Within a few months of his elevation, Basil was given a chilling sign of Michael's fickleness. While carousing after a horse race he had won, Michael responded to the flatteries of a new acquaintance, a boatman, by inviting the fellow to remove Michael's royal red boots and don them himself. Basil objected, and the emperor turned on him in fury. "I made you emperor," spat Michael, "and have I not the power to create another emperor if I will?"

Unlike Bardas, Basil did not attempt to convince himself that all would be well. He knew better. On a stormy September evening in 867, he was commanded to dine with the emperor at the Palace of St. Mamas, an imperial residence located across the Golden Horn from Constantinople. When Michael had drunk himself into his usual stupor, Basil slipped away to the emperor's bedroom, where he disabled the bolts that locked the door. He then returned and helped Michael to bed as he had done on so many previous occasions.

Soon he was back, accompanied by eight accomplices. The terrified courtier on duty was no protection for the sleeping emperor. One of the men slashed at the unconscious form and succeeded in hacking off both of Michael's hands. Then, while the bleeding emperor lay helplessly moaning and cursing on his bed, the conspirators debated whether they ought to finish him off. At length, one of them settled the matter, delivering the coup de grace. The assassins then rowed through the storm across the Golden Horn and in the night took possession of the Great Palace, to which they were admitted by an accomplice. Thus, with stealth and murder, began the second golden age of Byzantium.

Basil, a man without education or training, and only limited practical experience, had seized a troubled throne. Byzantium was on the verge of financial ruin, religious schism, and holy war with Islam. The government, no longer guided by Bardas, was nearly incapacitated by intrigue and incompetence, and Basil had mainly his common sense to guide him. Although from the first he was beset by palace plotters—not the least of whom were the angry relatives and friends of the dead Michael—he did enjoy broad support among the nobility, the senate, the army, and the citizenry.

This approval existed, despite the bloody circumstances of his assumption, because it was generally understood that the empire was in mortal danger. To begin with, Michael's wild excesses had emptied the treasury. Basil's most urgent task was to replenish it. But this was not to be simply a matter of heavier taxation. The Byzantine economy, for all its wealth of trade, rested on the bowed shoulders of the peasant farmer whose produce—wherever in the vast domain it was raised, whether grain or olives, sheep or cattle, vegetables, or grapes for wine—sustained the population. Already the lion's share of what the farmer had left over after feeding his family went to enrich neither himself nor the landlord, but the state. Whether used to support the army and the bureaucracy or as a reward for services to the throne, those funds were the primary source of wealth and power in Byzantium.

The spectacular ascent of Basil I from peasantry to the Byzantine throne resounded in legend long after his death in 886. Five centuries later, Sicilian monks produced a chronicle of the emperor's life illuminated with sketches, four of which appear here. Above, at left, a haloed Saint Diomedes appears at a monastery in Constantinople to urge its gray-bearded superior to welcome the young Basil; to the right, the saint's wish is fulfilled as the superior extends his hand to the destitute newcomer. Below, the red-cloaked Basil triumphs at the imperial palace, besting a vaunted Bulgarian wrestler by tossing him onto a table.

Although it had been many years since Basil had experienced at first hand the toils of a farmer, he surely remembered that the most feared and hated figure in the Byzantine world was the imperial tax agent. The methods of collection were more often than not high-handed and arbitrary, and the frequent result of such attention was ruin. The farmers suffered other afflictions as well. Devastating waves of crop disease and drought, grasping provincial officials, sudden invasions by enemies, all posed dire threats to the peasants' well-being and indeed to their lives. Natural disasters were regarded as acts of God and borne with stoicism, but taxation and corruption were presumably under the emperor's control, and therefore, they were bitterly resented.

The grim conclusion of Basil's relationship with his patron, the emperor Michael, is portrayed above in two scenes. At left, Basil—whose halo indicates that he has risen to the position of co-regent—receives whispered word that Michael has designs on his life; at right, a henchman dispatched by the alerted Basil delivers the deathblow to Michael. Below, after the deed, Basil assumes sole possession of the throne, ready to dispense justice in a stern yet evenhanded manner.

Basil approached the problem with both urgency and justice. Instead of raising taxes, he strove to make their collection fair and uniform. He dealt severely with venal officials and greedy landowners while doing everything possible to ensure that no poor farmer was driven from his land by taxation. The new emperor made sure that the rate of taxation was expressed in clear figures so that the taxpayers could understand what was expected of them. He also began a monumental revision of the Justinianian Code. Three centuries had passed since the Byzantine emperor Justinian I had recodified Roman civil law, and revisions were now clearly in order.

In a relatively short time, imperial coffers were replenished and the population noticed a distinct improvement in the quality of government. But there were still shadows across Basil's path, and one of the darkest was a crisis of religion.

Little more than two decades before, during the regency of Michael's mother, Theodora, the Church had emerged from a wracking schism precipitated by a movement known as Iconoclasm. Its adherents had declared that the widespread use of religious pictures—icons—in worship amounted to idolatry. For a time, the Byzantine emperors had sided with the Iconoclasts and had participated in wholesale destruction of religious art and artifacts. But the respecters of icons had eventually won out, and in 843, a council of reunification had put an end to the strife.

With religious images back in favor and a great demand for new works to replace those destroyed, Byzantium experienced a glorious resurgence of art. It would be called the Macedonian Renaissance, in honor of Basil and his descendants. And it would be distinguished by a fusion of Western and Eastern styles, a blending of the rich classicism popular in Greek cities with the austere reserve favored by Syrian and Anatolian monasteries. This rebirth would find its highest expression in the fabulous mosaics that would be applied to virtually every church and monastery in the empire—most conspicuously and spectacularly Hagia Sophia in Constantinople.

Yet although the Iconoclasts were defeated, serious problems remained. As so often in the past, they revolved around the exercise of power. The patriarch and his bishops shared with the emperor and his ministers a common goal: the further expansion of the dominions and population of the holy empire. But the clerics did not always approve of the behavior of the emperor, and they sometimes opposed him, even though he had the power to appoint or dismiss a patriarch. And there was intense missionary competition between the Eastern church centered in Constantinople and the Western church ruled from Rome; both were trying to win converts among the Slavs, for instance. When patriarch and pope disagreed, the confusing issue arose of who

1	WAREHOUSES	10	BOUKOLEON HARBOR
2	SOPHIA HARBOR	11	MESE (MIDDLE STREET)
3	FORUM OF CONSTANTINE	12	PRISON (SITE OF ANCIENT BATH)
4	THE SENATE HOUSE	13	HAGIA SOPHIA
5	CHURCH OF SAINTS SERGIUS AND BACCHUS	14	PATRIARCHAL PALACE
6	CHURCH OF SAINT EUPHEMIA	15	NEA CHURCH
7	HIPPODROME	16	OLD BARRACKS
8	IMPERIAL BOX	17	CHURCH OF SAINT IRENE
9	IMPERIAL PALACE AND GARDENS	18	POLO GROUNDS

By the ninth century, Constantinople, conceived in the image of Rome, had surpassed that city to become the hub of Christendom. Its teeming harbors and markets supported a diverse through the Roman-style Forum of Constantine and past the Hippodrome, dominated by obelisks from ancient Egypt and classical Greece. If those landmarks recalled past empires, however,

populace united by civic pride, which rose to a peak when campaigning emperors returned triumphant. The victors would parade down the arcaded Mese—a street lined with shops—
the royal precinct at which the procession ended told of a new imperium based on faith. Across from the palace grounds rose the Hagia Sophia, where emperor joined patriarch to worship.

could chastise or excommunicate whom. The question could not be easily answered.

An uneasy truce between religious and secular leaders had prevailed during Michael's reign until the patriarch Ignatius, outraged by a scandalous love affair involving the caesar Bardas, had refused the great man communion. Infuriated in turn, Bardas had accused the patriarch of some imaginary plot, had sent him into exile, and in 858, placed in his stead a favorite intellectual, a layman named Photius—the patriarch who was to lead Constantinople's spiritual defense against the Russians two years later. The new patriarch, supported by imperial power, took office, but was regarded as a mere usurper by Rome. In short order, the dispute deepened into schism. Pope Nicholas I in Rome declared Photius and his supporters excommunicated; the Eastern church responded by declaring Nicholas deposed from the papacy and anathema to the Church.

At this point, Basil had seized the throne and swiftly decided to bring an end to the quarrel. With no reason to maintain an ally of the murdered Bardas, the new emperor summoned a church council at which Photius was deposed and Ignatius was recalled. By 870, religious peace had been restored, Basil had a patriarch on whom he could depend, and relations between the Byzantine and Roman churches were settled, at least for a while.

What remained unsettled, however, was the holy war with Islam, which had been raging off and on since 634, when the Muslims had first burst forth from Arabia and invaded Byzantine territory in Syria. In the more than two centuries since then, the Arabs had greatly reduced the size of the Byzantine Empire in the Middle East, North Africa, and Europe. Basil was determined to seize the initiative in this age-old conflict. During the 870s, he continually attacked an Arab world that was in considerable disarray because of internal dissension. Simultaneously, Basil engaged the infidels in Asia Minor and in Italy and the central Mediterranean. The emperor proved to be victorious in the east, but not notably so in the west, where he lost the strategically important island of Malta and the great city of Syracuse on Sicily. The capture of Syracuse by the Arabs in 878 was a tragic and hideous affair, involving a siege of nine months that saw the inhabitants forced to eat grass, the hides of animals, bones ground up in water, and even the corpses of their fallen comrades. Epidemic followed unrelentingly the ravages of famine, and by the time the Arabs launched their final

In land battles as in naval warfare, Byzantine forces made fresh use of ancient techniques. The illustrations at right appeared in a Byzantine manual of siegecraft from the time of Basil II that drew on texts by contemporaries of Alexander the Great. Indeed, one of the machines portrayed—the so-called turtle *(second from right)*, designed to shield men from fire as they stormed a tower—was employed by the Assyrians as early as the eighth century BC. Such venerable tools of war posed a new threat with the introduction of Greek fire, which could be propelled over enemy walls from the ramp of a mobile siege tower *(far left)*, for example, or injected through a breach in the wall with a huge bellows *(second from left)*. Some of the contraptions sketched in the manual, such as a giant bow drill for boring holes in a wall *(far right)*, would have been difficult to deploy. Conversely, one of the most practical methods of taking an enemy fortress did not lend itself to illustration. Before committing men and machines, shrewd Byzantine generals heeded the advice of the ancient Greek strategist Philon and tried to bribe the opposing commanders. "Succeed in getting them on your side," Philon noted, "and you are sure of victory."

assault, most of the populace of the once great city had already succumbed to death.

Nevertheless, Basil somewhat increased the overall possessions of Byzantium during this energetic decade, all the while preparing his eldest son, Constantine, to succeed him as emperor. Basil was determined to found a dynasty, and not merely for reasons of self-fulfillment. Great harm was done the empire, he believed, when the succession was contested or attended by a radical change. It seemed to him that stability—that most prized of attributes in the Byzantine world—would best be served by making provisions for the orderly passage of power from one emperor to a like-thinking family member.

Although he had three other sons—Leo, Alexander, and Stephen—Basil always assumed that Constantine would be his heir. The boy had been borne by his first wife, Maria, before the imposed marriage to Eudocia, and Basil devoted himself wholeheartedly to Constantine, while maintaining only a distant relationship with the three younger children.

No child likes to be rejected, and for Leo it resulted in strong feelings of hostility, made worse by the machinations of one of Constantinople's master intriguers. In a remarkable demonstration of resiliency, the deposed patriarch Photius had worked himself back into favor at Basil's court, eventually being assigned the duty of tutoring Leo. And when the patriarch Ignatius died of old age in 877, it was Photius who replaced him. Then Photius reached even further; he fostered the alienation of Basil and Leo, possibly hoping to maneuver one of his own relatives into the line of succession. So cleverly did he plot that at one point Basil actually imprisoned his son for three years on charges of treachery.

In 879, tragedy struck the imperial household. Constantine died, and with him, Basil's dreams. Basil had made Constantine co-emperor in 869 when the child was scarcely ten. In later years, Constantine had campaigned with his father against the Arabs, clad in golden armor and mounted on a white charger. A state marriage was planned to the daughter of Louis II, one of the heirs of Charlemagne who ruled part of that Western emperor's now dismembered realm. Perhaps Basil had hoped that one day Constantine might rule over a united East and West. But now Constantine was dead, at the age of twenty, the possibilities of his future forever unrealized, and his father was deranged by inconsolable grief.

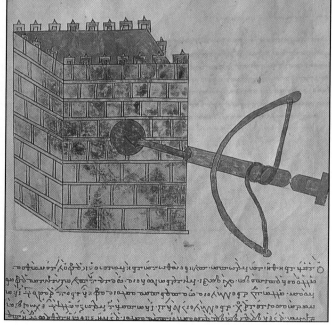

Basil ruled for seven more years. During that entire time, he was despondent, unable to accept the loss of his favorite son. He left to others the affairs of government, while he himself spent his time idly hunting. While at that pastime in August of 886, Basil suffered a bizarre accident. A huge deer cornered by the hunting party impaled the emperor on its antlers and carried him off, the stag's points being somehow caught under Basil's belt. A servant chased after them and succeeded in freeing the emperor by severing the belt, but Basil was fatally injured and died of internal hemorrhaging nine days later.

The man known as Basil the Macedonian was gone, but his stamp had been firmly impressed on the Byzantine Empire, and a son—not the one he had had in mind, but a son nonetheless—was ready to carry on.

Leo was crowned Emperor Leo VI at the age of twenty, and he reigned with vigor, if not with notable success, for twenty-six years until his death in 912. In theory, he shared the throne with his younger brother Alexander, but in practice he ruled alone while his less serious sibling pursued a life of pleasure. The new emperor of Byzantium was a different kind of ruler from his father. But the differences were more of style than of substance. Where Basil had plunged boldly ahead, Leo was more of a meticulous organizer; where the father had been renowned as a general, the son was known as Leo the Wise for his prolific writings and orations. Their aims were the same, however, particularly in the area of law. One of Leo's highest priorities was to bring to completion the sixty-book codification of the law commenced by his father. Collectively, with some handbooks Basil had published as an interim measure, this highly significant work became known as the Basilics and provided not only the principal body of Byzantine law, but a foundation for such later legal systems as France's Napoleonic Code.

One of Leo's first acts as emperor—as it had been for his father—was to depose the patriarch Photius. But where Basil had acted primarily to resolve a problem of state, Leo's motive was bitterly personal. He knew that the scheming Photius had been responsible for his imprisonment and took his revenge as soon as he could. The hateful old man soon died in exile, but if Leo imagined that he would henceforth be free from churchly interference, he was sorely mistaken. Relations between emperor and patriarch remained stormy.

The problem arose in part because Leo's wives kept dying. His first, chosen for him by Basil, passed away in 897. After a few months as a widower, Leo married his longtime mistress, but she died less than two years later, posing grave problems for the emperor. The Church permitted a second marriage under certain circumstances but had long absolutely forbidden a third. Civil law had been more lenient until Leo himself, a few years before, had brought it in line with church doctrine.

Yet Leo was without a male heir. The Macedonian dynasty was threatened with extinction after its second generation, and Leo followed his father in fervent belief that dynastic succession was essential to stability. With so much at stake, the emperor managed to get patriarchal permission to marry once again. But his new bride died

Like the Greeks of old, the Byzantines prided themselves on their swift galleys, known as *dromons,* or "racers." The typical ship of the imperial fleet *(model, left)* carried three sails, two banks of oars, and a crew of up to 300 men. A ram was used to shear the oars or puncture the hull of enemy vessels—the same tactic employed so skillfully by the ancient Athenians—but the chief weapon of the Byzantine navy was of more recent design. A volatile substance called Greek fire, whose precise formula would never be revealed, was ignited and pumped out of tubes protruding from the ship's forward platform. As suggested by the illustration below, the flamethrowers could also be operated with deadly effect from small merchant vessels, which were sometimes called on to defend Constantinople when the fleet was away.

in childbirth the following year, and the infant, a boy and heir, did not survive.

Leo lost all interest in marriage until 905, when his beautiful young mistress, Zoe Carbonopsina, gave birth to a male child. By now Leo had appointed an old friend, Nicholas Mysticus, as patriarch, but Nicholas stood firm in his duty to the Church and forbade the marriage. Desperate to make his son his legitimate heir, Leo struck a bargain with the patriarch: He would send Zoe away if the baptism of the boy were allowed to take place.

The son, Constantine, was duly recognized in January 906—and three days later, in an agony of love for Zoe and anger at the Church, Leo repudiated his agreement with Nicholas and called Zoe back to his side. He married her and proclaimed her empress, thereby triggering a church-state explosion that would reverberate all the way to Rome. Appalled, the patriarch not only refused to sanctify the marriage, but he took action to bar Leo even from entering a church; on two ceremonial occasions Nicholas personally turned the emperor away from the doors of Hagia Sophia.

Leo countered by appealing his case to the Roman pope Sergius, who was naturally delighted; the emperor thus seemed to be tacitly recognizing the pope's supremacy. After a suitably lengthy investigation, Rome applied its own, less stringent, views. The pope granted a dispensation and recognized the marriage. Leo then forced Nicholas to resign and banished him. The emperor had won, for the time being.

While all this was consuming Leo's energies, other events were taking place that would threaten not only the imperial succession but Byzantium itself. No sooner had Leo ascended the throne than a dispute with Bulgaria, a neighbor with whom the empire had been at peace for almost a century, degenerated into war.

The current Bulgar ruler was Symeon, a gifted and ambitious son of Boris I, the khan who had led his country into Christianity. The youth had been educated in Constantinople and had returned home convinced of two things: that Constantinople was the foremost city of the principal empire of the world and that he would one day be the master of that city and empire. Like his father, Symeon carried to his country samples of all the works of Byzantium, its art, its literature, its glorious architecture. The Bulgarian capital of Preslav was cast in the mold of a second Constantinople, with a newly constructed opulent palace where Symeon sat "in a garment woven with gold, a golden chain round his neck, girt with a purple girdle, his shoulders adorned with pearls, and wearing a golden sword."

Enthralled by the marvels of Byzantium, Symeon decided he would have to capture Constantinople and seat himself on the imperial throne. He shortly found an excuse to translate his desire into action. In 894, two merchants wangled from the court at Constantinople exclusive rights to the empire's trade with Bulgaria and immediately imposed stiff tariffs on Bulgaria's products. When Symeon protested and his representations were blandly ignored, he attacked, destroyed the Byzantine frontier forces, and marched toward Constantinople.

The sudden thrust caught Leo with the bulk of his forces committed to the war with the Arabs. In desperation, he appealed to a nomadic tribe known as the Magyars to attack Bulgaria from the rear, and when the wild Magyars fell on the Bulgarians, ravaging their northern provinces, Symeon was forced to negotiate an armistice. But he immediately went looking for an ally of his own and soon found one in the fierce Patzinaks, roaming the plains of southern Russia. Together they assaulted the Magyars and drove them from their Volga River domain to the plains of the Danube, where they later became known as Hungarians. Once again, Symeon hurled his forces against Byzantium. In 896, he was before the very walls of Constantinople and retired only after negotiating a punitive treaty, which required the Byzantines to pay him an annual tribute.

Meanwhile, Byzantine defenses against the Arabs were crumbling. One calamity followed another. After seventy-five years of continual fighting the last Byzantine stronghold in Sicily, Taormina, fell in 902, leaving all of the island in Arab hands. The fleets of Islam ranged the Mediterranean and Aegean virtually unchallenged, pillaging coastal cities at will. And two years later, in 904, the Arabs dealt the empire a particularly devastating blow.

A large Muslim naval force under a renegade Greek admiral called Leo of Tripoli sailed up the Aegean coast and attacked Thessalonica, which apart from Constantinople itself was the richest and most important city still controlled by the Byzantines after centuries of losses to the Muslims. For three days the battle raged, and then Arab landing parties took the city, sacked it, and butchered many of its inhabitants before sailing away laden with loot. Stunned and dismayed, the Byzantines now faced the ever-alert Symeon of Bulgaria, who prepared to annex Thessalonica for himself. That catastrophe was prevented only when the emperor Leo ceded extensive lands in southern Macedonia and Albania to the Bulgarian kingdom. It was an act that effectively united all the Slavonic tribes of the Balkans under Symeon's scepter and set the Bulgarians on the course to empire.

Obviously, the Byzantine Empire could not long endure such debacles, and Leo applied himself to restoring his military fortunes. With great determination, he energetically rebuilt his fleet, which soundly thrashed an Arab armada in the Aegean a

Woven in a palace workshop at Constantinople in the ninth century, the silk at right displays imperial eagles on a faded purple ground. Such majestic Byzantine silks were coveted in the West; this one shrouded the remains of Saint Germain at Auxerre in France, while another showing a triumphant emperor in his chariot *(opposite, bottom)* was found among Charlemagne's effects at Aachen. The Vatican, for its part, harbored a splendid silk portraying the Annunciation, with Mary and the angel encircled by a ring of flowers.

An Uncommon Cloth

The rich fabric of Byzantine life owed much of its luster to silk. From this sheer thread spun by the larvae of moths came purple garments to cloak the emperor, festive banners to herald holidays, and shrouds to cocoon the dead.

All this was made possible by the storied trade route that linked Byzantium to China. Most of the silk woven in Constantinople in the ninth and tenth centuries was imported from China, although some was cultivated locally thanks to Christian monks who had smuggled silkworms out of China in the sixth century. Equally important to the Byzantine silk trade was a horizontal loom of Chinese origin *(opposite, top),* furnished with treadles to speed the weaving of complex patterns. Thus equipped, the workshops of Constantinople became the envy of the world. A corps of imperial weavers and dyers met the needs of the palace. In the evenings there, ladies thronged the brightly lit House of Lamps to shop for the finest silks. The emperor's own silk wardrobe was unrivaled: During processions, he would stop at booths along the way and don new patterns to delight the crowd. Even when the imperial gloss of Byzantium began to fade, the wearing of silk remained a proud habit in Constantinople, as a Spanish merchant who visited the city in the twelfth century remarked. "All the people look like princes," he marveled. "Everybody is dressed in silk, purple and gold."

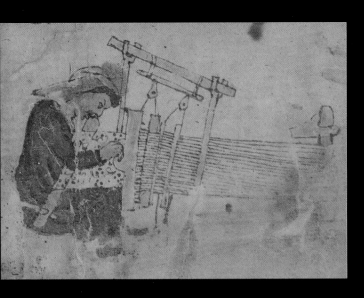

A woman seated before a horizontal loom draws the machine's comblike reed toward her to tighten her fabric in this Byzantine illustration at left. Barely visible near her feet is the treadle mechanism, connected by pulleys to wooden heddles rigged to raise or lower sets of long warp threads according to the pattern. Such an arrangement freed the operator's hands to pass the shuttle between the warp threads and draw the reed—reducing the time and tedium involved in weaving intricate designs.

little more than a year after the sacking of Thessalonica. In subsequent years, the Byzantines doggedly pursued the enemy eastward, successfully attacking not only Cyprus but even Syria.

Yet Leo had little time to enjoy this success before he was once again humbled; this time his humiliation was delivered by a massive Russian fleet that seemed to appear out of nowhere, as had the earlier Varangian attackers four decades before. The Rus anchored before Constantinople while their emissaries, led by a prince named Oleg, went ashore to announce their demands. When they departed, they took with them a series of highly favorable trade agreements. Worse still, in 911, an enormous Byzantine fleet failed in an attack against the Arabs on Crete. And while limping homeward the battered vessels were caught and crushed by another Arab fleet under the command of the infamous Leo of Tripoli.

The harassed Leo VI died that year, 912, and the throne passed to his reprobate brother Alexander, who himself died just thirteen months later, having managed to disrupt the government and embroil the empire in another war with the Bulgarians in that short time. At this perilous juncture the crown passed to Leo's seven-year-old son Constantine. It was precisely the situation Basil had feared—no male descendant was ready to assume rule of the Byzantine Empire, and the power of the throne became available to others. There followed a chaotic, decades-long period of regencies, pretenders, and military rulers during which the Macedonian dynasty continued in name only—that is, somewhere in the imperial palaces there was to be found a direct descendant of Basil.

Warfare with the Bulgarians was virtually continuous, and although Symeon never managed to breach the walls of Constantinople, his armies defeated the Bzyantines in battle after terrible battle. So awful was the carnage at the river Achelous in Thrace in 917 that a visitor to the site at the end of the century could write that "even now one can see heaps of bones" where the Byzantine army "taking to flight was ingloriously cut to pieces."

Constantinople was in anarchy in 919 when a savior strode forward, like Basil, from the ranks of the commoners. He was Romanus Lecapenus, the son of an Armenian peasant. Romanus's cleverness and military abilities had won him the high rank of admiral in the Byzantine navy. Then he deposed the dowager Zoe as regent and married his daughter to the young Constantine. Having paid the necessary amount of lip service to the legitimate dynasty, Romanus promoted himself first to the rank of caesar, then ultimately to co-emperor.

Before long, in 924, the Bulgarians were once more pounding at the gates of Constantinople. But this time, Symeon found in Romanus a man as ambitious and as hard as he. The two met in an historic confrontation under the walls of the city. Symeon gained almost nothing. Romanus understood that for all the Bulgars' victories, they could not conquer Constantinople. The Byzantine emperor therefore wisely acknowledged the Bulgarians' suzerainty over the territory they controlled, agreed to continue the payment of annual gifts, and recognized the Bulgarian ruler as an emperor. However, there were to be no further territorial concessions, and certainly there were to be no ties of marriage to the Macedonian dynasty, as Symeon had so long hoped and desired.

Three years later, in 927, still burning to possess the throne of Byzantium, Symeon died. His son Peter, a quiet, practical man, saw no point in continuing the contest and immediately concluded a peace with Constantinople that would last for forty years, during which the fires of Bulgarian expansionism would lie banked and glowing.

The greatest problem confronting the formidable Romanus would not yield to armed might. It was the unraveling of the social and economic fabric of the realm. In the half century since the death of Basil, the rich landowners and powerful provincial officials had been without restraint or conscience. Enormous estates and immense fortunes had been assembled by confiscating the property of poor farmers—many of them soldiers whose reward for loyal service was a small plot of land. Their suffering became intense in 933 when a brutal winter was followed closely by widespread famine. In their distress, many of the owners of small farms were forced to sell out to wealthy landlords.

Romanus, like Basil before him, understood full well that the security of the empire rested on the peasant farmer. "The small holding is of great benefit," he wrote, "by reason of the payment of state taxes and the duty of military service; this advantage would be completely lost if the number of small holders were to be diminished."

Romanus enacted laws sharply restricting the acquisition of land by the rich—who, he said scornfully, had "shown themselves more merciless than hunger or pestilence." And he saw to it that those forced by famine to sell their land had a preferential right of repurchase. But these measures encountered stiff opposition from provincial officials, many of whom were also landowners or relatives of landowners. Moreover, large numbers of peasants themselves objected. High taxes and uncertain crops had caused many peasants to prefer the lives of serfs, under the protection of powerful landlords, to that of independent but beleaguered farmers. It was not uncommon for peasants to give their plots of land to an overlord, simply to rid themselves of the responsibility.

Nevertheless, Romanus pursued his goal of land reform and went on to build hospitals, distribute food during times of famine, and construct extensive public works. Yet for all his noble efforts, he could never truly rally his people behind him. Byzantines great and small regarded their emperor as a usurper and reserved their affections for the young Constantine, known as Constantine Porphyrogenitus, or "Born in the Purple."

This attitude was characteristic of the profoundly conservative Byzantines, particularly the urban classes, who were closest to the unseemly power contests in Constantinople and most aware of foreign enemies. The typical Byzantine was a lover of lengthy and detailed ceremonies—at court, in church, within the family—that imposed a blessed order on every occasion. Above all else an individual was expected in all circumstances to remain calm and act in a reserved, orderly way. There were minutely prescribed procedures for composing paintings, decorating churches, and making speeches. Monks knew how often they were to bathe (once a month, unless ill), and all subjects understood when to weep (as frequently as possible, at least once a day). If there were stark contradictions, such as a general love of carousing that accompanied the worship of moderation, the bawdy humor and frequent adulteries that coexisted with high standards of primness and chastity, the Byzantine was capable of ignoring them.

And for all the orderliness of life, any means was legitimate when it came to determining who was to be successor to the Byzantine throne. Thus, it was no great surprise when, in 944, a plan to depose Romanus was conceived and carried out. What came as a shock was that the agents of downfall were not supporters of Constantine, but Romanus's own sons. His eldest had died, and the remaining two,

71

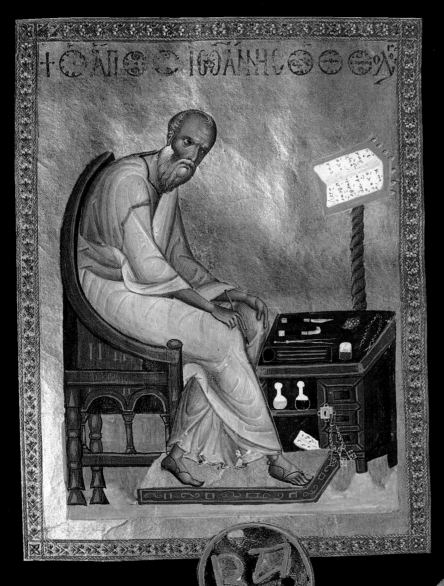

A Yen for Security

Constantinople, with its riches, relics, and secret documents, offered fine opportunities for robbers and spies. To deter such villains, Byzantine authorities relied on a pair of time-tested devices—seals, which served as proof of ownership and indicated whether a container had been tampered with; and locks, which confounded amateur thieves and, at the very least, gave pause to professionals. Often the two measures were combined. Attached to the Byzantine key chain below is the seal of the individual entitled to bear the four keys—a man named Basil. After locking a chamber or chest, Basil could seal the keyhole with wax or clay stamped with his unique insignia; then when he returned for inspections, one glance at the seal would tell him if all was well. A similar benefit was conferred by the device at lower left, a key and signet ring in one, bearing the monogram *(detail)* of Panaretus, who may have been an imperial steward.

Concern for the security of one's prized possessions was as intense among priests and scholars as it was among officials. The temper of the times was suggested by a Byzantine artist who added a revealing detail to his portrait of the evangelist John *(left)*—keys dangling from a lock on the saint's writing desk.

fearing that on the death of their aging father they would be excluded from power, decided to seize it. They actually kidnapped Romanus, carried him to a monastery, and forced him to take monastic vows. But before they could dispose of their brother-in-law Constantine, they discovered that Romanus had been their only supporter. They were arrested, on Constantine's order, and summarily condemned to share the monastic life with the father over whom they had hoped to ascend.

In the winter of 945, having been nominal emperor for thirty-three of his nearly forty years, Constantine VII assumed real authority for the first time. His exclusion from power had not been entirely repugnant; he had inherited from his father, Leo the Wise, a consuming love of literature and history but less of his father's aptitude for government. Constantine left a legacy that would reflect great honor on him and would be highly prized by succeeding generations. A gifted writer and avid scholar, he drew together the work of the finest intellects of his era. He compiled a handbook of Byzantine ceremonies, an encyclopedic description of the geography and history of the imperial provinces, a summary of existing knowledge about foreign lands and peoples, and a biography of his grandfather, Basil I, among many other works. Believing that the past could guide the present, he fostered a vast program of codification dealing with all aspects of life and government; his scribes produced manuals on several subjects, including agriculture, diplomacy, ethnography, antiquities, laws, and military strategy.

Constantine was also an accomplished painter. Palace gossip, probably exaggerated, had it that his father-in-law was so stingy that Constantine had to sell his paintings to keep himself in funds. Whatever the reality of the situation, Constantine became as emperor a patron of the arts, stimulating an empire-wide outpouring of thoughtful writing and exquisite decorative art. Goldsmiths, jewelers, and enamelers strove to surpass each other in the creation of objects that astonished with their complexity and beauty.

The splendor with which Constantine surrounded himself awed an ambassador from Italy called Liudprand of Cremona, who recorded his experiences in Constantinople. Liudprand was ushered into one of the emperor's throne rooms in the fall of 949. He wrote later that his attention was first riveted by a bronze tree whose branches were decked with mechanical birds that "uttered various cries according to their species." The enormous throne was flanked by golden statues of lions that "beat the ground with their tails and roared with open jaws and moving tongues." And the most spectacular part of the display was yet to come.

"After I had made a triple obeisance to the emperor, with my face to the floor," Liudprand continued, "I looked up and found he had meanwhile changed his clothes and was sitting on a level with the roof. How it was worked, I could not imagine."

Liudprand went on to remark on the emperor's obvious generosity. To celebrate the Feast of Palms, it was Constantine's habit to ceremoniously present a payment in gold to his vassals, and the Italian ambassador was an amazed witness to this wondrous Byzantine event. "A table was brought in, which had upon it parcels of money tied up in bags, according to each man's due. The recipients then came in and stood before the king, advancing as they were called up by a herald. The first to be summoned was the marshal of the palace, who carried off his money not in his hands but on his shoulders, together with four cloaks of honor. After him came the commander in chief of the army and the lord high admiral of the fleet. These being of equal rank received an equal number of money bags and cloaks, which they did not carry off on their shoulders but with some assistance dragged laboriously away."

Next, recorded Liudprand, came twenty-four controllers, each receiving twenty-four pounds of gold plus two cloaks, and a great number of patricians who each went away with twelve pounds of gold and one cloak. And thus it went, down through the knights of the sword, the ranks of chamberlains, treasury and military officials, and other functionaries, all receiving their share, be it six, five, four, three, two, or one pound of gold. The boon-giving commenced at six o'clock one morning and continued for three entire days.

At one point, as Liudprand was marveling at the proceedings, the emperor sent a chancellor to inquire how the ceremony struck him. Liudprand boldly replied: "It would please me if it did me any good." At which, wrote the Italian, "the emperor smiled in some confusion and motioned me to come to him. He then presented me with a large cloak and a pound of gold coins: a gift which he willingly made and I even more willingly accepted."

Absorbed by his books and such splendid ceremonies, Constantine relied on diplomacy in foreign affairs and was blessed with a period of relative peace along the empire's frontiers. The truce with the Bulgars continued. The conflict with the Arabs proceeded, of course, but fitfully, with neither side gaining any significant advantage. After Constantine's death in 959, his son Romanus II succeeded to the Byzantine throne. His rule lasted for a brief three years. When Romanus died suddenly, at the age of twenty-four, the Macedonian dynasty once again receded into the background, technically continuing in the persons of Romanus's two infant sons while the real power was exercised by a succession of military rulers. The first of these was Nicephorus Phocas, scion of one of the empire's most powerful aristocratic families and architect of the empire's most resounding military triumphs of recent history—the wresting of Crete from the Arabs in 960-961 and the devastation of the Arab forces along the empire's eastern border.

Here was a man who wanted to become a monk but loved war too much, who was of aristocratic birth but rejected the courtier's finery and grace in favor of a soldier's rough garb and coarse tongue. He was not immune to ambition, however, and when he saw his chance for supreme power he appropriated Romanus's throne and the late emperor's beautiful young widow.

He must have impressed the empress with the force of his character, for he seems to have been an unattractive sort physically—at least according to the Italian Liudprand, who had returned to Constantinople. (Liudprand's reactions may have been colored by the fact that he did not like the mean quarters to which a personage of his rank had been assigned.) "He is a monstrosity of a man," wrote the Italian, "a dwarf, fat-headed, and with tiny mole's eyes; disfigured by a short, broad, thick beard half going gray; disgraced by a neck scarcely an inch long; piglike; in color an Ethiopian, and as the poet says, 'you would not like to meet him in the dark.' "

Warming to his task, the acid-penned Liudprand described a ceremonial procession through the city. "As Nicephorus, like some crawling monster, walked along, the singers began to cry out in adulation: 'Behold the morning star approaches; in his eyes the sun's rays are reflected; Nicephorus our prince, the pale death of the Saracens.' And then they cried again: 'Long life, long life to our prince Nicephorus. Adore him, ye nations, worship him, bow the neck to his greatness.' " Sniffed the Italian: "How much more truly they might have sung: 'Come, you miserable burnt-out coal; old woman in your walk, wood devil in your look; clodhopper, haunter of byres, goat footed, horned, double limbed; bristly, wild, rough, barbarian, harsh, hairy, a rebel, a Cappadocian!' ''

Whatever his looks might have been, Nicephorus turned out to be a paradoxical ruler. For all his common manner, this deep-dyed aristocrat turned a harsh hand against the poor. His predecessors, Nicephorus announced, had been biased toward the peasants and had thus violated their responsibility to treat all subjects equally. To rectify the imbalance, he watered down the laws restricting the acquisition of small farms by wealthy landowners.

Nicephorus had sworn to end his days in a monk's cell, worshiping God and eschewing all power, possessions, and human entanglements. Instead, he found himself possessed of limitless wealth, absolute power, and a lascivious young wife—but denied communion by an outraged patriarch, who, reassured by his early devotion, had helped him to power. As a consequence, Nicephorus became an implacable enemy of the Church, most especially the monastic movement that he had at one time planned to join.

At the same time that he unleashed the landowners, he restricted and condemned the accumulation of church lands, which, he asserted, contradicted holy vows and transformed monastic life into ''an empty theatrical performance, bringing dishonor on the name of Christ.'' Nicephorus ordered the monks to leave the cities and go into the wilderness, forbade the establishment of new monasteries or the enlargement of old ones, decreed that bishops could be appointed only with his personal consent, and started confiscating the property of the Church.

But in one thing he was entirely consistent. He was not only a soldier, but a devout soldier, unswerving in his dedication to what he regarded as a holy war with Islam. There was no more important mission in his life than the destruction of the infidel Arab, and it was a duty for which he was eminently fitted. In 969, his army conquered Antioch, the rich Syrian city that had been wrested from Byzantine control 300 years before. Arab power in the northeastern Mediterranean was shattered, and part of Syria was once more a possession of the Byzantine Empire.

In the same year, Nicephorus's wife fostered a plot that ended his life. He was followed by first one and then another general with imperial ambitions, but by 976, the older of Romanus's two young sons had developed ambitions of his own. The young prince named Basil was possessed of a powerful will, an aptitude for war and statecraft, and an increasing distaste for the idle life to be found at court, which his younger brother, Constantine, relished to the fullest.

Basil now stepped forward to assume the throne in his own right, but to secure his claim he had to fight savage battles over a number of years against a series of would-be usurpers. And even when he seemed to get the upper hand over his domestic enemies, the Bulgars saw to it that his troubles did not cease. Their current ruler, named Samuel, challenged Byzantine supremacy throughout the Balkans. In 986, Basil II launched an expedition against the upstart Bulgarian empire but suffered a humiliating defeat. And upon his return to Constantinople, he found his leading

A fertility amulet showing the Greek monster Medusa, her head writhing with snakes, attests to the enduring power of pagan lore in Byzantium. The inscription invokes the "grace of God," while that on the reverse side calls on the womb of the woman wearing the amulet to remain tranquil and retain its life-nourishing blood. According to legend, the blood of the slain Medusa was used by the fabled healer Asclepius to revive the dead. Such myths and the charms they spawned were attacked by the Church; one prelate warned that using fetishes to treat the ills of the body might render the patient "even more sick of the soul."

domestic opponent, a general by the name of Bardas Phocas, in open revolt and supported by some of the empire's leading families and highest military officers.

In the spring of 988, Phocas approached Constantinople with a large army. The general positioned half his force at Chrysopolis, on the Asia Minor side of the Bosporus, and sent the other half against Abydos, at the southern end of the Dardanelles, in order to cut off supplies to the capital prior to a direct attack. The rebels were confident of success. Although he had been on the throne for a decade, Basil II was still widely regarded as young and inexperienced—and had he not just shown himself inadequate in the face of the Bulgars? But Basil II had depths of perception and will that his enemies did not appreciate.

Seeing the strength of the insurrection and realizing he was doomed without help, he had appealed to the Russian prince Vladimir. The Russians had no love for the aggressive Bulgarians and saw strong advantages in an alliance with Byzantium. And so it happened that Basil was able to ride out from Constantinople at the head of an army reinforced by 6,000 seasoned Russian troops and launch a stunning attack on

the divided rebel army. First he crushed one half of it at Chrysopolis, then turned his deadly attention to the other half at Abydos. The second battle was decisive. As the waves of valiant Varangians attacked with Basil in the forefront, Bardas Phocas suddenly appeared in the lines and personally aimed a thrust at Basil. His sword missed, and the general fell dead, apparently of a heart attack. The struggle was ended. The rebels fled and were cut to ribbons by the Varangians.

There remained only the fulfillment of a bargain with the Russians. In order to win Vladimir over to the Byzantine cause, Basil had agreed to the marriage of his sister Anna to the Russian prince, who in turn had promised that he and all of his people would undergo conversion to Christianity. But after the crisis had passed, the thought of a woman born to the purple becoming the wife of a distant pagan ruler seemed much too extravagant a price

The irrepressible empress Zoe *(above)*, who liked to concoct perfumes when she was not weaving strategems, enlivened Byzantine affairs for more than two decades following the death of Basil II. The daughter of Basil's successor, Constantine VIII, she took the throne after her father's brief reign and outlasted two husbands—Romanus III, who died mysteriously in his bath, unmourned, if not in fact undone, by Zoe; and Michael IV, her lover at the time of Romanus's death. After Michael's death in 1041, Zoe was dispatched to a convent by his nephew, only to return to the palace in triumph after a popular uprising. Then in her sixties, Zoe took a third husband, Constantine IX *(left)*. Taking their cue from the pragmatic empress, the court artists who fashioned this mosaic of her last consort on the walls of the Hagia Sophia simply substituted Constantine's features for those of an earlier husband.

to pay, and Basil made no effort to fulfill his part of the bargain.

When a powerful Russian army advanced into the Crimea, however, Basil was recalled to honor, and the marriage took place. Despite the reluctance with which the bargain was consummated, it resulted in a firm and long-lasting alliance between the majestic old empire and the vital young kingdom. It turned out, furthermore, to be a substantial victory for Basil, adding as it did considerable luster to the empire and, especially, the suddenly enlarged Church.

Basil took no time to savor his victories. Sadly, he had become incapable of pleasure. Thirteen years of grinding struggle had transformed him from a carefree young prince into a grim, embittered man who was unable to enjoy anything. Reserved and suspicious, the emperor had no time for courtly ceremonies or personal graces, only for the subjugation of those he perceived as his enemies. Among these he counted the wealthy families who had supported Bardas Phocas in the civil war. They now came under his baleful gaze.

The laws laid down by the emperor Romanus to restrain the voracious acquisition of peasant lands by the rich landowners had been unenthusiastically enforced by some administrations, amended by others, and most often ignored altogether. Basil II issued a decree of unmistakable vehemence, startling in its scope: All property acquired by the wealthy from the poor contrary to Romanus's laws, at any time during the seven decades since they had been promulgated, was to be restored to its former owners without any expectation of compensation.

Nor was Basil finished. By law, when a landowner failed to pay taxes, the debt fell on the neighboring farmers—the village community was held collectively responsible. In practice this applied only to peasants, because the rich, who in any case were more capable of paying their taxes, were often excused from them by some favor gained at court. Basil reversed the situation; henceforth, the rich would be the ones held responsible for delinquent taxes.

The nobles raised howls of protest, but in truth, they did not have much to fear. In the far-flung Byzantine Empire, issuing decrees was one thing, administering them another, and the great families were well versed in avoiding unpleasant duties and payments. What is more, Basil was unable to focus his full attention on enforcement of the laws, preoccupied as he was with another old foe.

This was Samuel of Bulgaria, who had defeated Basil once. Samuel would learn the effectiveness of Basil's dogged determination. "Basil II did not conduct his wars like most other emperors, who set out in spring and returned home late in summer," observed a contemporary chronicler, "for Basil, the time of return was decided by the achievement of the objective." He had not bested his domestic enemies at a single coup. Through the years, he had learned the advantages of patience, and he was not in the least deterred when his battles with the Bulgarians dragged on for years without a definitive decision.

Not only was Basil up against a capable adversary in Samuel, but he could never take his eye off the ever-opportunistic Arabs. Whenever they attacked, Basil would leave the Bulgarians to campaign in Syria or Armenia. Inevitably, Samuel would advance in the Byzantines' absence, whereupon Basil would return and restore his lines. Slowly, relentlessly, Basil chipped away at the flanks of the Bulgarian empire, reducing it a sliver at a time, gradually closing a set of Byzantine pincers. Through another thirteen years of brutal warfare, Basil maintained his initiative and at length, in the summer of 1014, drove Samuel's battered army into a narrow pass in the mountains located around the upper Struma River.

There Basil achieved his final, terrible victory. The Byzantine pincers closed on the Bulgarian army, and the surviving troops, perhaps 14,000 in number, were taken prisoner. Samuel himself escaped to the city of Prilep. He was followed by the awful retribution of Basil, who returned Samuel's army to him there.

In pitiful groups of 100 men, the Bulgar remnants stumbled down the road to Prilep, passing in ghastly review before their monarch and commander. They were blind. Their eyes had all been put out—one man in a hundred being left with one eye to lead the sightless legions home. Samuel, surveying the awful scene, was overcome by the horror of it all and collapsed unconscious on the ground. Two days later the ruler of Bulgaria lay dead.

Basil, known forever after as "The Bulgar-Slayer," completed the subjugation of the Bulgarian empire and then proved to be as moderate in governing his former enemies as he had been merciless in subduing them. But subdue them he did, and the result was the restoration of the entire Balkan peninsula to the dominion of the Byzantine Empire.

Basil pushed even farther during the decade after the final defeat of the Bulgars, taking up the sword against the Arabs once again, hammering the frontiers of Byzantium southward and eastward into Syria and Mesopotamia. Under his aegis the great empire extended from the Adriatic to the Caucasus and from the Danube to the Euphrates. Basil was preparing to head westward again, to lead a massive campaign against the Arabs of Sicily, when on the fifteenth of December, 1025, after reigning for forty-nine years, he died.

The greatness of the Macedonian dynasty and the Byzantine Empire expired with him. On his deathbed, being without descendants, Basil conferred the imperial crown on his aged brother Constantine, who had whiled away four decades in sloth and who now applied all the vast resources of the empire to the satisfaction of his many desires. Constantine, recorded a scornful scribe, wished only "to pursue his merely voluptuous way of life as the absolute slave of gluttony and lust, and to indulge without reflection in the amusements of the Hippodrome, the table, the chase, and games of hazard."

Thus, by a curious and unfortunate quirk, the preoccupations of Michael III—that long-ago, wastrel emperor whose unruly horse had led to the founding of the Macedonian dynasty—once again dominated Byzantine affairs. Constantine soon died without a male heir, and the government passed into the uncertain hands of his two daughters. In the years to follow, all the powers ranged against the Byzantine throne would run riot, and anarchy would unbind and convulse the land. Byzantium itself would survive for another four centuries, but the upheaval marked the end of the house of Basil the Macedonian and the passing of the brightest years of the empire that dynasty, founded by a peasant, ruled.

As fervent Christians and as inheritors of the proud Greek artistic tradition, the Byzantine people harbored a profound devotion to the sacred images that served as expressions and objects of their faith. The feeling ran so deep that no power on earth could eradicate it. That fact was borne home to Emperor Leo III in 730 when he decided to embrace Iconoclasm—a movement that condemned the worship of holy images as idolatrous. Leo announced his stand by ordering soldiers to tear down a majestic statue of Christ that crowned a gate at the entrance to Leo's palace in Constantinople. Word of the emperor's order spread quickly through the populace, and a crowd of angry women soon gathered at the gate, where a soldier perched atop a ladder was about to remove the icon. In the ensuing melee the women managed to overturn the ladder, sending the soldier toppling to his death. The leader of the protesters was said to be a nun by the name of Theodosia, who later perished in the Hippodrome for her convictions.

Many others risked death in the century to come for their devotion to icons—an attachment that proved particularly tenacious in monasteries and convents, where praying to sacred images was a hallowed tradition. A number of such bastions held firm against the Iconoclasts even as splendid painted and mosaic icons were being effaced in Hagia Sophia and other Byzantine churches. In time, the Iconoclasts began to lose their moral grip.

Early in the ninth century, Emperor Leo V defended his adherence to the policy in strictly selfish terms, contending that "all the emperors who have acknowledged and worshiped icons met their death either in exile or in war; and only those emperors who did not worship them died a natural

death on the throne and received glorious burial in the imperial sepulchers." This dubious argument was laid to rest on Christmas Day in 820, when Leo V died an unnatural death: He was assassinated.

The last emperor to oppose icons was Theophilus, who came to power in 829 and faced ill-disguised opposition to his stand from his own wife, Theodora. On one occasion, a court jester informed the emperor that he had glimpsed Theodora kissing a small icon in her chamber. Confronted by the emperor, Theodora coolly denied the charge, but later, after Theophilus's death, she made no attempt to mask her convictions. As regent for Theophilus's young heir, she used her power to put an end to Iconoclasm. Its official demise in 843 occasioned widespread rejoicing and was celebrated in churches then and every year thereafter on the first Sunday in Lent as the Feast of Orthodoxy.

Theodora's initiative marked the dawn of a proud new age for sacred art and architecture in Byzantium. As exemplified by the splendid monastery church of Hosios Loukas *(pages 80-83)*, built at Phocis, near the Gulf of Corinth, the finest shrines of the era confirmed the age-old Greek belief in the power of the artist to make the divine spirit visible. The church buildings themselves were cruciform, reminding all who entered that Christ's sacrifice was the foundation and framework of their faith. At the nexus of the cross rose a lofty dome, its interior decorated with a mosaic showing the stern features of Christ the Pantocrator—ruler of the universe. Worshipers who made so bold as to glance up at that visage from the nave during services might have experienced some of the mixture of dread and joy that Jacob spoke of in the Book of Genesis: "I have seen God face to face, and I have survived."

As if to relieve the congregants of the great weight of that presence hovering above them, the sanctuary at the front of the church—where priest and deacon prepared the bread and wine for communion—was crowned by the reassuring image of the Virgin with the infant Jesus *(above)*, a vivid emblem of Christ's willingness to descend from on high and share in the lot of humankind. The painful price Christ paid for that act was, of course, the theme of the Eucharist itself, which reenacted the offering up of his body and blood with such vividness that some worshipers were reluctant to come forward and accept the host. The solemn nature of the communion rite was underscored by the deacon, who stood at the portal of the sanctuary, between a panel painted with the icon of Christ and another representing the Virgin, and with chalice in hand sent forth the call to the congregation: "Approach with the fear of God and with faith."

A Tribute to a Saint

Built around the year 1000, the church of Hosios Loukas (Saint Luke) was a product of the thriving Byzantine monastic movement. Most citizens of the empire contributed to that movement, either by offering money or goods or by spending part of their lives in a monastery or convent.

In Byzantium as in the Far East, it was common for older people to join a holy community as a way of preparing for the hereafter. But the true champions of the faith tended to embrace the ascetic life at an early age. The tenth-century saint for whom the church of Hosios Loukas was named left his parents at the age of fourteen to join other monks. In time, a longing for solitude led him to a rugged hillside in Phocis where ancient Greeks had once worshiped the goddess Demeter. There Luke passed his last eight years in a small cell, visited now and again by pilgrims and acquiring a reputation as a healer and prophet. Before his death in 943, it was said, he foretold the liberation of Crete from Muslim control. When that prophecy was fulfilled in 961, Luke's reputation was bolstered, and powerful patrons offered their support to the monastic community that had grown up around the saint's rude dwelling. By one account, the church that arose there drew support from Basil II, the ruler who led the Byzantine Empire to new heights. A fitting monument to power and piety, the building projected a fortresslike solidity, relieved by a host of graceful arches that left ample space for windows to throw light on the sacred designs within.

Wrought of stone, brick, and tile, the exterior of Hosios Loukas reveals the building's symbolic plan— a cross within a square, with the cross defined by the gable transepts projecting from the central dome. Although Hosios Loukas has endured as a shining example of Byzantine church architecture, similar shrines were constructed wherever the Eastern Orthodox faith took hold, including Russia and the Balkans.

A mosaic of the Virgin and Child (center) links the heavenly heights of Hosios Loukas to the sanctuary below. Fronting the sanctuary are icons of Mary and the mature Christ.

A Cosmic Arrangement

The artists who decorated the Hosios Loukas and other Byzantine churches of the era followed a scheme laid out during the reign of Michael III, whose mother, Theodora, had put an end to Iconoclasm. This scheme represented the Eastern Orthodox view of the cosmos—from the roof of heaven to the terrestrial plane below. As universal overlord, the Pantocrator *(below)* was situated within the dome, encircled by angels. The prophets who had risen to heaven were arrayed below, between the windows at the dome's rim *(left)*. Farther down, near the crown of the apse, sat the Christ Child in the lap of the Virgin, whose immaculate conception had brought him to earth. Closer to ground level, mosaics and frescoes portrayed crucial moments in Christ's earthly career, each linked to a Church festival. The most solemn of those was Good Friday, when worshipers contemplating Christ's death on the cross *(right)* could contrast that suffering figure to the commanding presence in the dome and ponder anew the central paradox of their faith. As the Orthodox Liturgy expressed it: "He who suspended the earth in the waters now hangs upon a piece of wood."

Christ meets death on the cross, having entrusted Mary to his disciple John *(right)*.

This somber image of Christ the Pantocrator, from a church at Daphnē, is similar to the one that dominated Hosios Loukas before an earthquake dislodged it.

84

Pearls border the enameled figures of the crucified Christ and various saints and angels on this gilded book cover crafted in Constantinople around 900 to hold a sacred text. The back of the cover is inscribed, "Lord help thy servant Maria," an apparent reference to a wealthy Byzantine woman who was cured of a serious illness and donated this prize in gratitude to a shrine honoring the Virgin.

Treasures of the Sanctuary

Short of taking vows, the surest way for a Byzantine dignitary to earn spiritual credit was to lavish gifts on the Church. The results of such patronage can be seen here: liturgical objects that must have dazzled monks and layfolk.

The appeal of these precious articles was only enhanced by the ceremony surrounding them. The gospel book, whose cover might be studded with gems or pearls *(far left)*, was paraded by a deacon down the nave at the start of the communion service. Before the gospel was read, a cantor took up his psalter *(following page)* and sang the prescribed passages, with each verse eliciting a chorus of alleluias that reverberated in the dome. The preparation of the bread was a moment of high drama, as the priest pierced the leavened loaf in imitation of the Roman soldier who had thrust his lance into Christ's side. The priest later divided the loaf and arranged the segments on the gleaming paten *(below)*. The bread was then dipped in the wine held in the chalice *(left)* to reunite body with blood before the host was offered to communicants "for the remission of sins and for life everlasting."

Saints and angels raise their hands in gestures of blessing on the rim of this chalice fashioned of enamel, pearls, gilded silver, and cut sardonyx. The inscription identifies the donor as the "orthodox emperor Romanus," probably Romanus II, who took the throne in 959 and presided over the reconquest of Crete—a victory over Islam that occasioned gifts of thanks to the Lord.

This alabaster paten fringed with gems has a portrait of Christ at center, surrounded by his words: "Take, eat, this is my body." Like the other objects shown here, the paten was among the Byzantine works deposited in the treasury of San Marco in Venice—many of them brought there by Latin crusaders who sacked Constantinople in 1204.

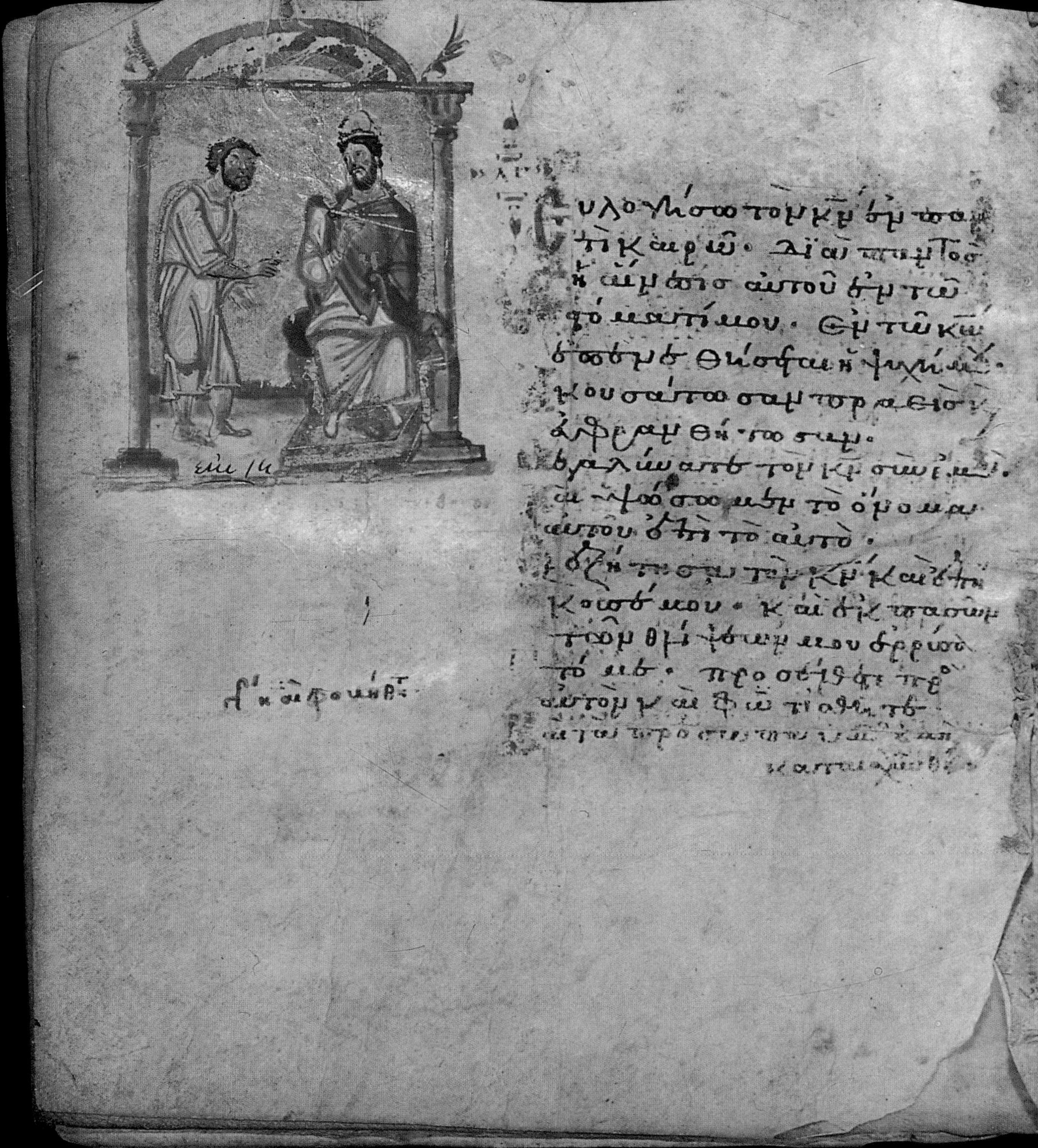

These pages from a Byzantine psalter, which served as a hymnal during communion services, are decorated with scenes from the New and Old Testaments. At right, Christ celebrates the Last Supper with his disciples; at left, David stands before the throne of a hostile king, feigning madness to win his freedom. According to tradition, David celebrated his escape by composing the Thirty-Fourth Psalm, transcribed here in Greek. Among its verses is a line that would have had special meaning for communicants in a Byzantine church as they stood surrounded by sacred images and prepared to receive the host: "O taste and see that the Lord is good."

ουτος ο πτωχος ὀκέ κρα . . ε
καὶ ὁ κς ͅ εἰσήκουσιν αὐτου·
καὶ ἐκ πασῶν τωῶν θλίψεων
αὐτοῦ· ἔσωσεν αὐτόν·
παρεμβαλεῖ ἄγγελος κυ
κύκλω τῶν φοβουμένων ·
καὶ ῥύσεται αὐτούς ·
γεύσασθε καὶ ἴδετε ὅ
ὁ κς· μακάριος ἀνὴρ ὃς
ἐλπίζει ἐπ αὐτόν· φοβή
θητε τὸν κν πάντες οἱ ἅ
γιοι αὐτοῦ· ὅτι οὐκ ἔστιν ὑ
στέρημα τοῖς φοβουμέ
νοις αὐτόν· πλούσιοι ἐπτώχευ
σαν καὶ ἐπείνασαν· οἱ δὲ ἐκ
ζητοῦντες τὸν κν οὐκ ἐλατ
τωθήσονται παντὸς ἀγαθοῦ·
δεῦτε τέκνα ἀκούσατέ μου·
φόβον κυ διδάξω ὑμᾶς·

THE DISTINCTIVE JAPANESE

Late in the year 882, the Japanese imperial court received word that a delegation from the Manchurian kingdom of Parhae had crossed the sea from the Asian mainland and landed in northern Japan. Delighted by this opportunity to impress their distinguished guests with the manifold glories of Japanese civilization, imperial officials immediately began planning what would be a memorable state visit. Orders went out to repair roads, bridges, and government buildings along the route the visitors would travel. Gifts of food, wine, and winter clothes were dispatched to the 105 men from Parhae. When the preparations were complete, emissaries were sent to escort the foreigners to the imperial city, Heian-kyō, meaning "capital of peace and tranquility." (Later the name would be shortened to Kyoto—simply "the capital.")

The fourteen-year-old emperor Yōzei, his ministers, and the robed and powdered nobles who composed Japan's ruling elite could scarcely wait to show off the cultural attainments of their society, which, like that of Parhae, owed much to the older civilization of China. As the envoys traveled south toward the capital, Heian court musicians rehearsed on their flutes, zithers, and other instruments for the reception galas; and decrees were issued specifying the robes to be donned by even the most minor officials.

Poetry, which the Japanese aristocrats adored and elevated beyond all other art forms—to them, it was the language of the learned—would figure prominently in the diplomatic sessions, as it did in the richly ceremonial life at the Heian court. Fully half of the officials chosen to meet the Parhaeans were accomplished poets. Like Pae Chong, leader of the visiting dignitaries, they composed their poetry in Chinese.

Five months after their arrival in Japan, the foreigners finally appeared on the broad, willow-shaded boulevard that led to the imperial palace in Heian-kyō. After a few days' rest, they presented gifts and a message from their king in a grand ceremony attended by the entire court. At a subsequent banquet, Emperor Yōzei honored the visitors by granting them ranks in the elaborate hierarchy of his court, together with the appropriate costumes. Now properly robed, the envoys were feted with food and entertainment, including rice wine, loquats from the emperor's table, and a performance by 148 female dancers.

The state visit happened to coincide with one of the many festivals the Japanese celebrated, the iris festival, during which houses were decorated with iris leaves and courtiers wore garlands of iris blossoms to ward off evil spirits thought to cause sickness. Unfortunately, it was raining on festival day, and for the visitors' comfort, the formal rites were transferred indoors. However, later in the day, everyone braved the downpour and ventured outside with umbrellas to watch horse races and archery contests. A few days after these festive events, the mission's commercial business was transacted, a trade of goods that included such items as furs (tiger and bear among them), honey, and ginseng from Parhae in exchange for Japanese silk and brocade.

There were cultural exchanges, as well. Sugawara no Michizane, a gifted poet who would later ascend to great political power, led Japanese bards in what amounted to a friendly contest in the extemporaneous composition of poetry. The contest rules specified the number of characters per line (five or seven) and the number of couplets (four or six) and established particular themes. All told, Michizane reported afterward, the hosts and their guests produced no fewer than fifty-nine harmonious poems. The versification was more than a pleasant interlude; it was a part of the official interchange between the two countries.

After a two-week sojourn, the Parhae delegation said their good-byes, and Michizane lamented the leave-taking in a typically graceful poem: *At this farewell gathering, why does nightfall seem so slow in coming? / Because only then will we be able to shed tears in the privacy of darkness.*

The visit of the Parhaeans spoke volumes about the Japan of the age. In a time of barbarism and upheaval, of pillage and slaughter throughout much of the eastern and western world, Japan was a gentle, peaceable kingdom, an island of stability and tranquillity in the raging human seas. The four centuries between 800 and 1200, moreover, were a period of tremendous accomplishment for Japan, a time when its people at last stopped depending on outside influences as models for Japanese behavior and forged their own distinctive civilization.

Largely unhindered by foreign invaders or domestic strife for much of this era, the rulers and nobles of Japan developed a style and sensibility, a refinement of aesthetic taste, and a subtlety of manner and expression that set their culture apart from both its contemporaries and its successors. But if Japan was in many ways a brilliant society, its light cast an uneven glow. Form was often valued more than substance in the Heian world, and the common people who supported the aristocratic few counted for very little.

Japan's insularity contributed both to the peace it enjoyed during these centuries and to its singular cultural evolution. China, the colossus to its west, had influenced almost every aspect of Japan's higher culture prior to this time—its government and legal code, its language, literature, and religion. But formal contact between China and Japan withered in the ninth century, and the Japanese turned inward. Parhae, whose people were an amalgam of Korean and Manchurian ethnic strains, was for many years Japan's chief link to the Asian mainland, a region in tumult.

China's great Tang dynasty, which had brought the country to a shimmering eminence in the seventh and eighth centuries, began to totter in the ninth and finally collapsed in the first years of the tenth century. The vast empire fell into warring factions. For half a century, chaos reigned. Even after one warlord finally prevailed and established the Song dynasty in 960, Chinese armies were constantly embroiled in frontier wars with the Khitan peoples to the north and the Tibetans to the west.

In southeast Asia, the lands that ultimately would be known as Vietnam and Cambodia evolved distinctive cultures while sporadically battling each other and their neighbors. Annam—the northern

The Japanese monk and scholar Saichō, portrayed here on silk in the act of meditation, was living proof of Japan's cultural debt to China at the dawn of the Heian era. The scion of a wealthy family of Chinese origin, Saichō visited China in 804 as part of an official embassy to the Tang court at Changan. The trip proved a harrowing one: His party was first buffeted by a typhoon during the crossing, then caught in a snowstorm during the trek overland to the capital. But Saichō was rewarded for his pains. The wisdom he gleaned from Chinese teachers inspired him to found a powerful new Buddhist sect in Japan. Known as Tendai, it combined esoteric meditation techniques with the simple promise of salvation for all.

part of Vietnam—was dominated by China during the Tang years but eventually established its independence in bloody clashes with the Chinese and the small, sophisticated kingdom of Champa to its south. In Cambodia, the Khmer civilization supplanted the earlier culture of the kingdom of Funan and created a new nation called Kambuja, which ascribed its origins to the union of a hermit sage and a goddess. Kambuja dissolved into anarchy in the eighth century. But a Khmer leader eventually regained control and established the Angkor dynasty, celebrated for its magnificent temple architecture, which was exemplified by the towering spires and terraced grandeur of Angkor Wat.

Protected from the mainland turmoil by the isolating sea, Japan in this period would shift from a Chinese-style political structure to a home-grown system—but the change was gradual. Well into the Heian era, the Japanese modeled their government on the Chinese pattern of centralized authority, with a bureaucracy run by a corps of civil servants at least nominally chosen on the basis of merit. Yet in time, despite the best efforts of a few strong-willed emperors, a number of great noble families would slowly become the real masters of the island kingdom. Clustered around the emperor, these landed aristocrats, along with a new class of provincial warlords, were to dominate the imperial regime so thoroughly that the official government's influence would be confined largely to the capital, and the true ruler of Japan would be a provincial baron who shunned Heian-kyō altogether.

Yet while it endured, Heian Japan was a cultural triumph of surpassing magnitude. Absorbing its Chinese overlay, the country was to develop a distinctively Japanese aesthetic, discover new means of expression in its own language, literature, and art, and integrate the imported religion of Buddhism with Japan's own traditions of Shintoism.

In 793, an army of laborers began building a new capital to replace the old city of Nara as seat of imperial government. Emperor Kammu and his noble advisers had ordered the move. The winds of change were commencing to blow, and Kammu, the fiftieth sovereign in a line that traced its divine right back a millennium to the sun goddess Amaterasu, was sailing before the gusts. He had abandoned Nara in a move against the Buddhists. The religion had been introduced into Japan in the sixth century, and the power of its adherents had grown so much that they were now interfering with the conduct of government. The new capital, though only thirty miles away on the Yamato plain, would be largely free of the monasteries that had come to dominate the old capital. The city that rose by the Kamo River, on a plain punctuated by gentle hills and

In 793, the Japanese emperor Kammu commissioned a new capital called Heian-kyō, or the City of Peace and Tranquillity. The place (present-day Kyoto) was aptly named, for there members of the ambitious Fujiwara clan, sanctioned by the successive emperors, oversaw a central government that proved strong and stable enough to impose a degree of order on Honshū and the lesser Japanese islands for some three centuries. During this proud era, known as the Heian age, Japanese culture moved beyond its dependence on Chinese traditions to attain fresh heights of originality.

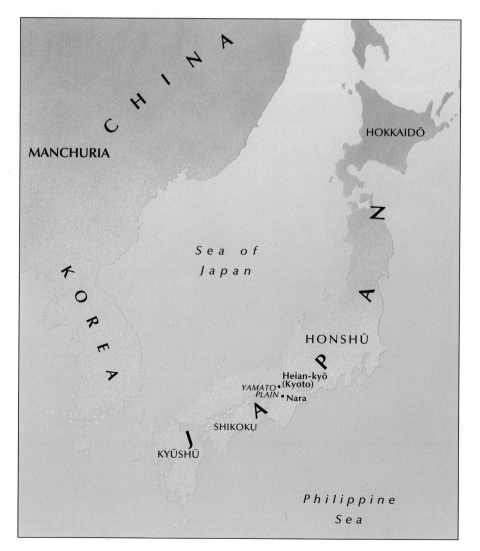

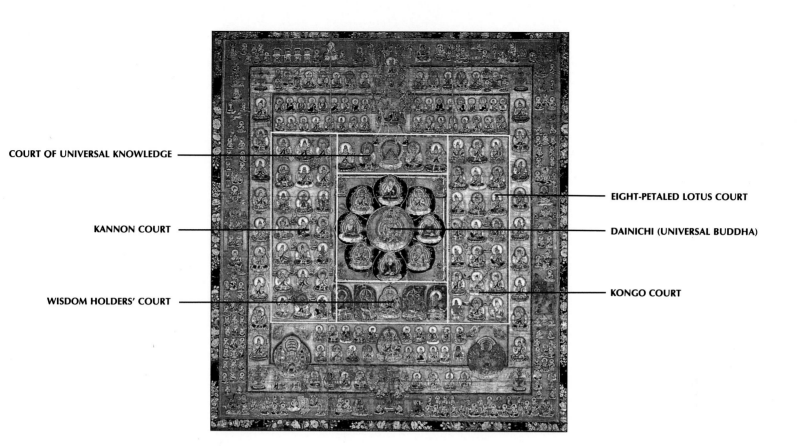

COURT OF UNIVERSAL KNOWLEDGE

EIGHT-PETALED LOTUS COURT

KANNON COURT

DAINICHI (UNIVERSAL BUDDHA)

WISDOM HOLDERS' COURT

KONGO COURT

A Map to Enlightenment

The Buddhist mandala at left, with its hypnotic array of heavenly beings, was among the sacred objects of Japan's Shingon sect, an order founded by the monk Kūkai after his return from the same mission to China that inspired the scholar Saichō. The devotees of Shingon relied in their meditations on certain holy sounds (mantras) and images (mandalas) that empowered them to commune with Dainichi, or the Universal Buddha. In this image, known as the Womb Mandala, Dainichi sits amid a lotus blossom at the center of the design. Surrounding him on the blossom's petals are four lesser Buddhas, who occupy the cardinal points, and four honored bodhisattvas—saintly beings who have chosen to remain part of the imperfect, physical world to help enlighten others. Bordering this central zone are subsidiary courts, outlined above, whose figures symbolize various emotional and intellectual aspects of the search for enlightenment. The Court of Universal Knowledge, for example, with its triangle of fire, represents the pure flame of understanding that consumes all illusions, while the Wisdom Holder's Court, occupied by wrathful kings, symbolizes the righteous indignation that protects truth seekers from evil. The figures in the Kongō Court to the right are manifestations of the Universal Buddha's supreme intelligence, while those in the Kannon Court to the left embody his mercy and compassion. The rest of the mandala is divided into similar, allegorical groups whose members are all expressions of the spirit of the universal being at center and thus resemble him closely; the small haloed figures at the outer fringe represent the various non-Buddhist deities that members of the Shingon sect honored as distant reflections of Dainichi's brilliance.

93

stretches of luxuriant forest, was designed for some 100,000 people and was a masterpiece of urban planning. Although Chinese influence was starting to fade, Heian-kyō, like Nara, was modeled generally on the Chinese capital of Changan and was meticulously laid out down to the last intersection.

Three and a half miles long by three miles wide, Heian-kyō was surrounded by a moat and a modest earthen embankment. In a nation without enemies there was no need for looming battlements, although thick walls did enclose the imperial palace grounds and the noblemen's mansions. Broad, tree-lined boulevards, numbered and symmetrically laid out, divided the city into 1,200 blocks of identical dimensions.

Two markets were included in the plan, one to serve the eastern section and the other the western part of the city. The scheme also set aside wards where various groups of artisans were to be concentrated. It allowed for only two temples, a limit dictated by continuing concern about the temporal power of Buddhist monks. Paradoxically, a Japanese belief that northeast was an unlucky direction was nullified when a monastery was erected on a hill a few miles to the northeast of the new capital; while wary of the monks, the imperial court was still willing to accept the protection they offered. A mile-long palace complex near the city's center included the emperor's residence, Shinto shrines, several halls where ministers convened, and the 170-foot-long Great Hall of State—a red-walled, multicolumned building topped with a roof of green tiles.

As Heian governmental structure evolved, the most exalted of the palace courtiers were the members of the Great Council of State. These included the prime minister and the ministers of the left, right, and center (bureaucratic titles indicating rank; the minister of the left was the most powerful and the minister of the center the least powerful). The council also included officers called the major, middle, and minor counselors, imperial advisers, and the controlling boards of left and right. (Later, after a noble family named Fujiwara ascended to a position of power, the Great Council's role was overshadowed by the extralegal positions of regent and chancellor, which became hereditary Fujiwara preserves.)

Below the Great Council in the Heian scheme of things came the eight ministries—central affairs, ceremonial affairs, civil administration, popular affairs, justice, war, treasury, and the imperial household. The next layer down was organized into bureaus—divination, medicine, and the court university, among others—which reported to the ministries.

Court posts were allotted in accordance with an elaborate code of rankings, and the rankings in turn were determined primarily by family status; lineage counted for a great deal more than ability. The top five ranks were reserved for the highest officials, who were permitted to have access to the emperor, while ranks six through nine were primarily clerks and other functionaries, with a few specialists in fields such as law, astronomy, or medicine.

Rank was everything among men at the Heian court. It conferred wealth—the top five ranks received income from land grants. It determined the color of a man's robe, the splendor of his residence, the type of carriage he had, and the number of outriders in attendance; it even mandated the number of folds in his fan—twenty-five for men of the first, second, and third ranks; twenty-three for men of the fourth and fifth ranks; and twelve for those at level six and below. Since women held no official positions, they were not involved in the system of ranks.

The wheels of Heian governmental machinery ground exceedingly fine. An imperial decree began as a proposal in the council of state, went to the emperor for approval and drafting in Chinese—until Japanese writing evolved—made a stop at the ministry of central affairs, and then passed to the scribe's office for copying. Next, it went back to the council of state and the emperor for further scrutiny, after which more copies were made and signed by the appropriate bureaucrats. Only then was the imperial seal affixed and the decree promulgated.

Kammu, the first of the Heian period's emperors, was ambitious and assertive. Besides commissioning the new capital, Kammu took additional steps to diminish the temporal influence of the Buddhists and concentrate authority in himself and his lay advisers. Though personally a devout Buddhist, Kammu promulgated edicts forbidding monasteries and temples from accepting land from peasants and from accumulating wealth in what might be deemed an unreasonable manner. Kammu also sought to shore up government land policy, which provided the regime's revenue through taxes on those who worked public land; one of the measures forbade the movement of farmers away from imperial fields to private, tax-exempt lands owned by monasteries or noble families.

During Kammu's reign the regime was engaged in one of the few wars of the whole Heian era. The enemy was the aboriginal Ainu, a people of puzzling origin whose racial characteristics made them resemble Europeans more than they resembled other East Asians. These fierce and independent tribes were concentrated in the northern provinces. They resisted all efforts to bring them to heel, and they had repelled a number of imperial expeditions aimed at subduing them. The government armies were composed mainly of peasant conscripts, who had no interest in fighting an implacable enemy far from home. But at last, Kammu commissioned an effective general, Sakanouye Tamara Maro, who shrewdly enlisted the aid of local landowners, and they in turn filled the imperial battalions with the men of their own families and their followers. These loyal forces finally subjugated the Ainu in a succession of bloody battles fought around the close of the eighth century. The triumphant Tamara Maro was rewarded with the impressive and descriptive title of Sei-i Tai-Shōgun, or "barbarian-subduing generalissimo."

With certain exceptions, the emperors who followed Kammu in the first half of the ninth century were less inclined to exert imperial power and quickly fell under the sway of the great families. They also displayed a propensity to abdicate rare among monarchs of any land or age, a custom that had its roots in the long-standing habits of Japanese life. For emperors and aristocrats, ceremonial and family responsibilities were so oppressively heavy that the heads of great houses commonly retired at an early age, to spend their later years free of crushing social obligations. Kammu's son, the emperor Saga, ascended to the throne in 809 and abdicated fourteen years later in favor of his younger brother, Junna, who in turn abdicated at age forty-eight after only ten years on the throne. Indeed, nineteen of the thirty-three Heian emperors gave up the throne voluntarily.

Emperor Saga's short reign was notable mainly for the establishment of an imperial police force to carry on his father's policy of centralizing authority. Otherwise, he exhibited a continued devotion to China as the fount of wisdom. Good government, he declared, depended on literature, and progress came about through learning. At this time, many Japanese aristocrats still saw China as the source of both. The career of the ninth-century scholar-politician Michizane, poet laureate during the visit of the Parhae envoys, was a case in point.

Michizane was born into a low-ranking noble family, but one with a reputation for academic achievement. Both his father and his grandfather were poets and scholars whose intellectual abilities earned them modest positions at court. A prodigy as a boy, Michizane prepared for the entrance examination at the imperial university by writing poems on different themes each day. At the university he studied Chinese literature, and after graduation he passed a qualifying examination for the civil service. One essay question asked him to ''analyze earthquakes,'' which he did by presenting the Confucian, Daoist, and Buddhist philosophical views on the subject; the examiners were not seeking a scientific answer. The Confucian view he cited, for instance, held that the earth shook when the emperor was wanting in virtue.

Beginning as a sixth-rank bureaucrat, Michizane served stints in several different agencies—drafting documents in one post, helping administer budgets and taxes in

Three scroll paintings illustrate the legend of the gifted Heian politician Sugawara no Michizane, who incurred the wrath of the dominant Fujiwara clan and was exiled from Heian-kyō to the island of Kyūshū in 901. At near right, rowers propel the banished Michizane *(seated, aft)* and members of his household toward Kyūshū as a soldier looks on from the shore *(upper right)* and a sea monster glares from the deep *(lower left)*. At far right, Michizane stands alone on a Kyūshū hilltop shortly before his death, facing the distant capital defiantly. Below, Michizane's angry ghost returns to Heian-kyō as a thunder god to torment his opponents with lightning bolts and an epic deluge. The tale of Michizane's revenge was spawned by actual misfortunes that befell the capital after his death and led authorities there to appease his spirit with posthumous honors.

another—before gaining a coveted appointment as professor of literature at the university. His severe and somewhat haughty personality earned him few friends, but he was admired for his learning and talent. It was while he was a professor at the university that he was summoned to help welcome the visitors from Parhae.

As an imperial official, Michizane could be called on to serve anywhere his superiors deemed appropriate, but it still came as a shock to him when he was named governor of Sanuki province in 886. Like most of the courtiers, Michizane regarded a term in the backward provinces as tantamount to banishment. Sanuki gave him his first exposure to the common side of Japanese life. As governor, he toured the province regularly to "examine the customs, inquire about the elderly, offer justice to the falsely accused, and look into the complaints of peasants." The experience had a powerful effect on Michizane. He expressed it, as always, in verse. "To whom does the cold come early?" he wrote. "To the child orphaned as an infant / His robe woven of kudzu vines is too thin for winter / He lives on greens hardly adequate to sustain him." The scholarly governor also complained that he was "surrounded by corruption like a swarm of dirty black flies."

Michizane's fortunes improved dramatically when he returned to the capital after four years in Sanuki. The emperor Uda, who had succeeded to the throne while Michizane was away, appointed him to the exalted office of chief chamberlain. Uda's predecessor had been controlled by Mototsune, one of the earliest of the strongmen who exemplified the power of the soon-to-be-dominant Fujiwara clan, but on Mototsune's death in 891 the new ruler saw a chance to reestablish the emperor's personal authority. Promoting Michizane, whom Uda admired as a learned man, was one means to this end.

In the decade that followed, Michizane scaled heights of power previously beyond a man of his relatively modest background. Two of his daughters married into the imperial family, a privilege limited to the highest-ranking aristocrats. At one point, he held six imposing titles simultaneously, and when he became middle counselor in 895 his influence equaled that of Tokihara, leader of the Fujiwara. With Uda's patronage, Michizane was now one of the two most potent individuals in the realm, and when Uda made the decision to abdicate in favor of his thirteen-year-old son,

Daigo, Michizane and Tokihara became de facto co-regents for the young emperor.

Then, suddenly, Michizane tumbled into disgrace. His position had begun to weaken after Uda's abdication, although he continued to gather honors and titles. But in 901, an edict issued by the emperor Daigo declared that Michizane had "deceived the former emperor with flattery and now intends to disrupt the imperial succession." Michizane's words were obedient, the decree said, but "his heart is rebellious." Michizane was assigned to a nominal provincial post—in effect, sent into exile.

The charge of rebellion was baseless. Michizane was brought down by the machinations of his Fujiwara rival and Miyoshi no Kiyoyuki, an old foe from his years as an academic. With a pliable youth on the throne, Tokihara no longer saw any need to share power, and Kiyoyuki may have begrudged Michizane's rapid rise beyond what was regarded as his proper station.

As an exile, Michizane was paid no salary and remained under house arrest. He lamented his fate in verse: *Demoted, I carried less weight than a mustard seed / Driven out, I was sent here with the speed of an arrow.* He died two years later at the age of fifty-nine. In a footnote to his remarkable career, Michizane's reputation was eventually restored by a subsequent and admiring emperor. The poet was posthumously elevated to senior first rank, the loftiest position in the Heian hierarchy, and in time he achieved that greatest of all honors: He was transformed into a Shinto god.

For all of this, the acquiescence of the Fujiwara clan was undoubtedly necessary, for their hold on the Heian emperors—established in the seventh century—continued into the eleventh. Marriage into the imperial family was central to Fujiwara strategy. The tactic depended on an abundant supply of Fujiwara daughters, who became the wives and consorts of emperors and their heirs. One eleventh-century Fujiwara patriarch was the father-in-law of four emperors and the grandfather of three more. Little wonder that the Fujiwara were able to monopolize the positions of regent when the emperor was underage and chancellor when he was an adult.

Their dominion reached full flower in the last of the tenth and the early eleventh centuries under a skillful leader named Michinaga. He was reputedly a lover of luxury, but he was also possessed of great physical and intellectual prowess, an accomplished horseman and a poet with a gift for "understanding the human heart"—always important at the Heian court. He was certainly not given to false humility or modest disavowals of his role. In an unabashed poetic tribute to himself Michinaga wrote, *This world, I think, is indeed my world / Like the full moon I shine, uncovered by any cloud.*

With the Fujiwara the true powers in the realm, the emperors were mostly reduced to ceremonial and ritual duties and to a role as exemplars of correct conduct. Daigo, the emperor who banished the unfortunate Michizane, advised the next emperor to drink little wine, control his temper, avoid noisy and turbulent people, speak only when necessary, and shun ostentation.

This final commandment was the hardest to obey, since the emperor's ceremonial function obviously mandated pomp. An account of a monastery dedication attended by Emperor Ichijō in 1022 notes that the monarch's arrival was heralded by a crescendo of drums, strings, and reeds. "Jeweled nets were suspended from the branches of the plants fringing the pond," the scribe recorded. "Boats adorned with gems idled in the shade of trees, and peacocks strutted on the island in the middle." Gold, silver, and lapis lazuli were strewn on the floor of the monastery's main hall. Dancers performed in a room suffused with incense. The evening ended in traditional fashion, the chronicler reported, when "the guests, becoming intoxicated, recited Chinese poems." Significantly, while the emperor was the guest of honor, the man who had ordered the monastery built was the Fujiwara leader Michinaga.

Not only was the Fujiwara family the most powerful family in Japan; it was by every measure the wealthiest. Noble families gained tax-free parcels of land through special dispensations from the emperors, who were of course under the Fujiwara thumb. As the great families acquired more and more land in this fashion, the government tax rolls steadily decreased, and income from the rice fields flowed into the noble houses rather than into the imperial treasury.

The provincial estates, known as *shōen*, in time became largely free from imperial control. Each shōen had an elaborate structure of managers and overseers who received a portion of the income from the land. Private landowners, including peasants with small plots, frequently "commended" their land to large estates, becoming in effect tenant farmers in exchange for protection and lower taxes.

The Fujiwara became so exceedingly land-rich that a dissident member of the clan claimed in 1025 that the "first family" had "not left even a speck of earth for the public domain." On the rare occasions when an emperor was emboldened to reverse the trend, the landed aristocrats, supported by their relations at court, simply defied the monarch or otherwise managed to thwart his will. By the end of the Heian period, the Japanese countryside was a patchwork of 5,000 shōen and government land had all but disappeared.

Although most provincial lords remained peaceable in those days, adventures into banditry and rebellion occasionally ruffled the placid surface of Heian Japan. A tenth-century chieftain of the Taira family—a family that would become even more troublesome later—led a five-year-long revolt that sputtered out when his allies abandoned him at a crucial moment. Another nobleman turned pirate and pillaged coastal areas with an armada of a thousand small boats before he was subdued.

Nor was lawlessness confined to the countryside. Robbery and other petty crimes were common in Heian-kyō, where in 1040 a thief had the audacity to break into the royal palace and make off with some items of imperial clothing. The Japanese criminal code demanded confessions, which were often encouraged by torture. The

His garments billowing as if to signal his pride, Fujiwara no Michinaga stands by the pond of his estate, admiring pleasure boats built for a forthcoming visit of the emperor. Michinaga, who wielded the real power behind the throne for three decades beginning around the year 1000, was something of a dandy: He once kept the empress and her ladies waiting while he had a new underrobe sewn because he did not want them to see him in the same outfit he had worn at a recent event.

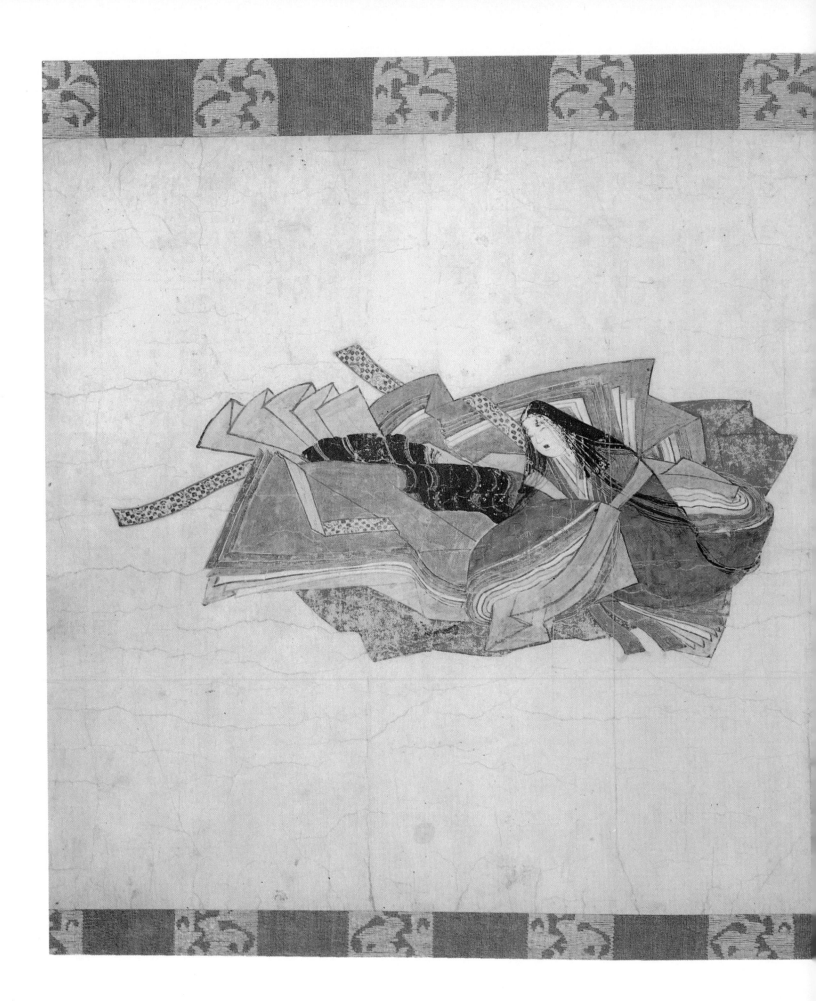

The Feminine Hand

"Once I wrote down in my notebook a poem that had greatly appealed to me," the Heian court lady Sei Shōnagon recollected. "Unfortunately one of the maids saw it and recited the lines clumsily. It really is awful when someone rattles off a poem without any proper feeling." The learned Shōnagon may have been offended by the awkward recital, but the very fact that the maid could read the poem was a tribute to the burgeoning literacy of Japanese women. While handmaidens were learning to decipher script, ladies of higher rank were honing their skills as writers. Several women at court—including Shōnagon herself, the novelist Murasaki Shikibu, and the poet Kodai no Kimi *(left)*—won lasting renown for their efforts.

The prominent role of women in the flowering of Japanese letters owed much to the development in the ninth century of a handy phonetic script called kana: a concise set of syllables derived from Chinese characters. Since this script could be acquired without lengthy schooling, it was deemed acceptable for women, while men were expected to master both kana and traditional Chinese writing, with its thousands of characters. Kana, as a bridge between the sexes, soon became the medium for love poetry, giving women a part in literary affairs. But the real breakthrough came when women at court began to use their training in letters to fashion prose accounts of the society they knew so well. The chronicles that resulted, notably Shōnagon's *Pillow Book* and Murasaki's *Tale of Genji*, exhibited a style that was as elegant and richly layered as the costumes of the day—and one that proved infinitely more revealing.

penalties were flogging, forced labor, exile, or death, but a contrite miscreant could usually escape punishment by pleading for the mercy of the court.

Heian Japan's contacts with the outside world were limited to diplomatic exchanges with China and Parhae and calls by Chinese traders at western ports. Relations between China and Japan were sensitive because the Chinese expected a deference that the island people were increasingly disinclined to offer, despite the fact that Japan still looked to China for books and ideas. A distinction between "Chinese knowledge" and "Japanese sense" began to appear in Japanese literature, a point underlined by stories showing clever Japanese outwitting their learned neighbors.

The Heian court dispatched two major missions to the Chinese capital in the ninth century, but in 894, on Michizane's recommendation, formal relations between the two nations were severed, not to be resumed for more than five centuries. The reasons were complex: Piracy in the Sea of Japan and political disruption during the late Tang period were among those cited, but the Japanese were also becoming more generally independent of China. Informal commercial visits by private traders continued, supplying the Heian-kyō aristocrats with the luxury goods they coveted. Imperial missions to Parhae continued until 926, when that kingdom fell to the aggressive Khitans, after which official contact between Japan and mainland Asia virtually ceased.

The Fujiwara family's grip on the reins of imperial government finally weakened in the middle of the eleventh century. The great sense of common purpose that had sustained the clan gave way to feuding factions. And biology seemed to fail the Fujiwara clan, which for some reason ceased producing strong baby boys to become emperors. It was at this time, in 1068, that an independent-minded young emperor, Go-Sanjō, succeeded to the throne. His mother was not a Fujiwara, and during his years as crown prince, his relations with the Fujiwara regent were marked by suspicion and acrimony—all of which stiffened the new emperor's resolve to govern without the Fujiwara hand resting heavily on his shoulder.

Go-Sanjō's declaration of independence took the form of a bold thrust at the heart of the noble families' wealth and power—the shōen. He established a land record office charged with investigating the claims of the gentry and the Buddhist temples to their vast holdings. Land without clear immunity to taxation was liable to imperial confiscation. Although this move met with only a limited amount of success, it did result in the abolition of some private estates and an increase in the lands under imperial control.

Go-Sanjō abdicated after four years and died a year later at the early age of thirty-nine. His son Shirakawa followed his father's example in accruing imperial power and reducing the influence of the Fujiwara. He achieved both goals by means of a novel system known as Insei, or rule by so-called cloistered emperors.

The system had its roots in the old custom of early retirement for the heads of aristocratic households, seen to great extent among Japanese sovereigns, so many of whom had tired rapidly and relinquished their burdensome thrones.

Yet in Shirakawa's hands, abdication became not a release, but an immensely potent political tool. He abdicated after fourteen years as emperor, but instead of slipping into honored obscurity, he placed a docile heir—a minor son—on the throne and continued to direct the imperial government from a retreat. As part of his scheme, Shirakawa took holy orders, which conferred sacred status and offered some protection against secular dangers. Most important, Shirakawa created a source of power independent of the maternal relatives of whoever occupied the imperial throne. In the

Genji sits with head bowed near the deathbed of the woman he loves. In the author's words, his "numbing grief made the world itself seem like a twilight dream."

A SAGA ILLUMINATED

In a certain reign there was a lady not of the first rank whom the emperor loved more than any of the others." So begins Lady Murasaki's *Tale of Genji,* a saga of Heian court life in which love contends time and again with the claims of rank and reputation. Murasaki's hero, Genji—the child of the emperor by his favorite lady—pursues his own romantic interests with a royal abandon, although he is prevented by his mother's low standing from succeeding to the throne. Instead, that honor falls to a boy who is regarded as the emperor's rightful heir—but who is in fact Genji's own son by his father's highest consort. Such complications abound in the novel, lending a dramatic intensity to the simplest encounters.

Some of that drama is conveyed here in a selection of twelfth-century paintings illustrating the novel. The scenes are filled with telling details—costumes and effects that reveal the richness of Heian court life. But the faces are masks. To peer beneath them, one must look to Murasaki's prose.

Her long black hair streaming down her back, one of Genji's wives—known as the Third Princess—lies desolate in her chamber after giving birth to a child by another man; her father, who has taken vows, sits in his monk's habit beside her cushion, while Genji waits in the foreground. In her shame, the princess has resolved to become a nun, the author notes, and her father has summoned priests to cut her locks: "And so they were ravaged, the thick, smooth tresses now at their very best."

Serenaded by a flutist, Genji sits with his back to a pillar across from his son the emperor, who has retired from the throne to live in peace. "It was late and the moon was high, and the young men played this and that on their flutes as the spirit moved them," Murasaki writes. "The emperor was delighted. His resemblance to Genji was more striking as the years went by. The emperor had chosen to abdicate when he still had his best years ahead of him and had found much in the life of retirement that pleased him."

As his wife steals up behind him, Genji's legitimate son Yūgiri kneels before a box of writing implements to open a letter from the mother of a woman he has been furtively pursuing. In the novel, his wife proceeds to snatch the note from his grasp, and Yūgiri acts the injured party: "Read it, if you are so curious. Does it look like a love letter? It seems rather common of you to want to." Yūgiri's ploy proves successful, Murasaki observes: "He did not try to recover the note, nor could she quite bring herself to read it."

Ladies of the court attend from behind a screen as the reigning emperor, dressed in flowing robes, plays a game of *go* with Kaoru—assumed to be Genji's son, but in fact the fruit of the Third Princess's illicit union. "There is something I might wager," the emperor remarks before the last game—a veiled reference to one of his unmarried daughters, whom he intends for Kaoru. After losing the game, the emperor makes clear his marriage plan by directing Kaoru to the garden: "Well, I will let you break off a blossom. Go choose one, if you will."

Two cousins united in marriage—Genji's grandson Prince Niou and his granddaughter Rokunokimi—awaken to look on each other for the first time in the light. The prince is delighted not only with his bride—whose hair flows alluringly "in a heavy cascade over her shoulders"—but with her comely attendants *(left)*, handpicked by the bride's father, Yūgiri: "Yūgiri knew that he had a demanding son-in-law to please, and his ingenuity in seeing that every detail was the best of its kind was astonishing (appalling, some might have said)."

In a tranquil corner of a troubled house, an attendant combs the hair of Nakanokimi *(left)*, who has emerged as the fickle Prince Niou's chief wife; facing her is her younger sister Ukifune, who looks at pictures illustrating a romance as another attendant reads from the text. Well aware that the shy Ukifune has just been subjected to Prince Niou's advances, Nakanokimi forsakes jealousy for compassion. As Murasaki sums up her thoughts, "She and Ukifune had lived apart over the years, but now that they had met, nothing must separate them. Yes, it was all very sad. The world was full of the most remarkable complications."

past, the Fujiwara were able to influence an emperor because his empress was usually a Fujiwara daughter. Now, power passed to the paternal side; an emperor who abdicated could continue to govern because the new emperor was his own son. By this ingenious means did Shirakawa effectively reign for forty-three years, until his death in 1129. In that time, he placed three different titular emperors on the throne. And those who followed as cloistered emperors continued to assert their rule for yet another sixty-three years.

In their assault on the Fujiwara regents, Shirakawa and his successors recruited their chief advisers from families that had previously labored in the shadow of the Fujiwara, notably a rough-and-ready provincial clan called Minamoto. In the year 1027, before Go-Sanjō's time, all but two of the twenty-four highest posts at court had been occupied by Fujiwara nobles, but by 1100, Minamoto aristocrats held half of the top positions. For all their self-aggrandizing ways, the Fujiwara had been notable patrons of learning. The Minamoto were not so intellectually inclined, and the emphasis on cultural attainment and knowledge at the imperial court diminished.

Nor were the Minamoto as clever in manipulating the emperors they served. Shirakawa and the other cloistered rulers remained relatively independent and greatly increased the royal coffers at the expense of the nobles. But it was merely a temporary revival. The period of cloistered emperors ended around the middle of the twelfth century, amid a new surge to power by the clans. This eventually brought about the demise of the singular, serene, and elegant era of the Heian court.

But it was a dazzling world while it lasted. "What can possibly equal the ceremonies performed in his majesty's presence on the occasion of the special festivals?" wrote Sei Shōnagon, an extraordinary Heian woman who won lasting fame for her literary work. In *The Pillow Book*, which she wrote at the end of the tenth century, Sei Shōnagon continued: "A bright sun shone in the peaceful spring sky, and in the garden in front of Seiryo Palace, mats had been spread out by men of the housekeeping office. Assistant officials of the emperor's private office placed little tables in front of each of the noblemen in attendance. One after another the guests took the bowl and, after holding it for a while, poured some of the wine into a thing called a *yaku* shell and drank.

"At this point," wrote Sei Shōnagon, "two of the dancers ran forward to start the first dance. They stood facing the emperor, with the sleeves of their robes joined in exactly the right way. The other dancers came out one by one, tapping their feet in time with the music. Having adjusted their costumes—the cords of their short-sleeved jackets, the collars of their overrobes, their headdresses, and the rest—they began dancing to the accompaniment of 'The Little Pines' and other such songs."

The author was enraptured. "I could gladly have watched them all day as they danced, moving their wide sleeves like great wheels," she wrote. "They made a most elegant picture as they glided gracefully away, their cloaks removed from one shoulder to let the sleeve hang down and the long trains of their glossy silk underrobes stretching out in all directions and becoming entwined in each other. Now they had gone, and I was left with the sad thought that there would be no more dancing that day." Grace and precision, elaborate attention to the most minute detail, poignance, beauty and melancholy—that was the style of the Heian court, a world inhabited by an elite who referred to themselves as "dwellers among the clouds."

The cloud-dwellers lived by the code of *miyabi*—courtly refinement—which, placed elegance and restraint among the principal virtues. It was a society that valued

Ceremonial occasions of great pomp and complexity abounded in the Heian court. Here, in a painting from a scroll describing annual functions at the palace, bearers of the royal palanquin stand among officers of the imperial guard (*left*) as the emperor emerges with two ladies wielding fans (*right*) to pay a New Year's visit to his father the former emperor. "What can compare with an Imperial Progress?" Sei Shōnagon asked in her notebook after one such event. "When the Emperor passes in his palanquin, he is as impressive as a God."

the subtle grace, the right color or scent or poetic couplet. The color of a sheet of writing paper and the way it was folded were freighted with meaning. So were precise shadings of etiquette, the intricate swirls of fine calligraphy, even the taste displayed in dressing. One court lady said of another's costume of multicolored silk robes—they wore as many as a dozen at once, drawn back at the wrist to display the blend of hues—that "it was really not very bad—only one color was a little too pale."

In personal appearance, the Heian ideal was a round white face—both sexes applied powder—and a tiny mouth. Men wore black headgear and affected little tufts of chin hair; women shaved their eyebrows, blackened their teeth, and wore their hair in long silky tresses. Courtiers of both genders favored loose, flowing trousers and silk robes and wore delicately scented perfumes, the blending of which was a highly cultivated art. Unattractiveness was unpardonable; Shōnagon advised ugly men to sleep only at night so no one would see them lying down, apparently in the conviction that they were even uglier in that position.

Religious and cultural ceremonies filled the court calendar. In a single month, the emperor presided over the Obeisance of the Four Directions, the Bestowal of Ranks, the Ceremony of the Blue Horses, the Feast of the Day of the Rat, and the Ceremony of the Poetry Dances, among other rites.

When courtiers gathered in a nobleman's garden for what was called a "winding water banquet," they took turns plucking a floating wine cup from a stream, sipping decorously, and reciting an appropriate poem. Heian life moved at such a languid pace that when a provincial uprising demanded a military response, the court debated for forty days before agreeing on a suitably auspicious time for the departure of a punitive force.

In their spare hours the courtiers enjoyed board games such as *go*, a Chinese import played with black and white stones, and also a form of backgammon that was played for money and was periodically prohibited by officials who frowned on gambling. They also indulged in dice games and a variety of verbal contests that gave them a chance to flaunt their erudition and knowledge of the Chinese classics. Aristocratic athletes in silk robes and lacquered hats played a type of soccer that involved keeping a leather ball airborne. They also vied in archery and one-on-one horse races, which could become strenuous since the object was not merely to outrun an opponent but to unhorse him as well.

The Japanese lacked the Chinese flair for cooking, and they apparently did not devote great energy to pleasures of the table. Food did not loom large in Japanese literary tradition. Rice was undoubtedly the staple, often eaten with vegetables such as sweet potatoes, carrots, radishes, or seaweed. Meat was generally shunned, in keeping with Buddhist principles. Fish, however, was permissible—boiled, baked, or pickled, but not raw as later Japanese would eat it. Main meals were eaten in midmorning and at about four in the afternoon. The beverage of choice was rice wine—tea was confined to medicinal use—and the contemporary chronicles suggest that the Heian enjoyment of sake frequently strained the bounds of decorum.

Members of the leisured class did not concern themselves with the passage of time; they were forever staying up till sunrise. They slept on raised and curtained platforms covered with mats and cushions, rested their wine vessels on low tables, and sat on the floor. Portable partitions and sliding doors divided rooms.

Poor roads and the danger of highwaymen made country travel precarious, reinforcing the popular notion that there was no reason to leave Heian-kyō anyway. But there were, of course, numbers of adventurous and ambitious nobles who actively sought appointments in the provinces, where they could grow wealthy with land. When they traveled about the countryside, it was with a party of guards, the nobles either on horseback or riding in an ox-drawn carriage. The carriages of the aristocracy were wonderfully ornate, and on ceremonial days they jostled for position and choked traffic on the avenues. The carriages of the imperial family and the highest-ranking ministers were protected from the elements by elaborate green gabled roofs, while humbler officials had to be content with palm thatch.

The formality that characterized so much of Heian society extended to the family circle, where notes and poems often took the place of conversation. Family loyalty and respect for one's parents were cardinal virtues. In a testament written for his descendants, a Fujiwara lord instructed them to tell their parents whatever they saw and heard and to "wait upon your father once every day." Outside the family, the noble instructed, "social intercourse, unless on a strictly formal footing, is to be regarded as dangerous, leading to jealousy, quarrels, and slander." Family members were to "prize gravity and solemnity" and "never give way to great anger."

Poetry at the Heian court was more than just the favored literary form; it was part of everyday social life and court ritual. The ability to compose verse was the sine qua non of civilized men and women; a failure of inspiration on certain occasions—the first snow of winter, an outing to the country—was a serious social gaffe. The recipient of a poem was expected to reply promptly in kind, and in the same imagery. Official business was not conducted poetically. Yet on one occasion, when the minister of military affairs wished to convey displeasure with his assistant, he did it in a verse replete with obscure references, precipitating a flurry of stylized poetic communiqués between the two.

Poetry was also the language of flirtation and seduction, and no one was more adept at this provocative and subtle blend of art and romance than the diarist Sei Shōnagon, who was lady-in-waiting for Empress Sadako, a Fujiwara noblewoman and a wife of the emperor Ichijō.

Shōnagon's *Pillow Book*, a loosely organized journal of vignettes, thumbnail portraits, and jottings, is among other things a vivid depiction of romance in her privileged world. Women were relegated to inferior status by both Japanese culture and Buddhist doctrine, and upper-class ladies were expected to remain largely invisible to all men except their fathers and husbands. Though permitted to own property, Heian women were educated only in poetry, music, and calligraphy, and their role was to obey their husbands and to bear their children. Yet none of these strictures seemed to hinder Shōnagon and the women of her circle, who moved casually from one dalliance to another without apology or guilt.

"Throughout the night one hears the sound of footsteps in the corridor," she wrote. "Every now and then the sound will stop, and someone will tap on a door with just a single finger. The man finally gives up, thinking the woman must be asleep; but this does not please the woman, who makes a few cautious movements, with a rustle of silk clothes, so that her visitor will know she is really there." In the assignation that ensued the man first had to coax the woman out from behind her "curtain of state," a six-foot-high partition that hid her from male eyes. Even then, in the nocturnal gloom of a Heian room a couple could make love without seeing each other.

Shōnagon, a scholar's daughter who may have been married at one time, was cheerfully open about her romances. When a man visited her, she wrote, "if it is at all possible I will keep him with me for the night." She judged her lovers by the elegance of their morning departure. "When he jumps out of bed, scurries about the room, tightly fastens his trouser sash, stuffs his belongings into the breast of his robe, and then briskly secures the outer sash, one really begins to hate him." When the empress Sadako heard that a man with an umbrella had been seen leaving Shōnagon's quarters, she sent the lady a drawing of an umbrella. Shōnagon replied with a sketch of falling rain and a couplet: *My name, though innocent of rain / Has long been spattered by unfounded tales.*

Marriages among Japanese aristocrats could be genuine love matches, or they could be arranged by their families through a matchmaker. The protocol included the inevitable exchange of poems and three formal visits by the young man to the home of his intended, with a presentation of rice cakes on the third night signifying formal religious sanction of their union. A feast and a simple service at the bride's house followed. Nobles had a principal wife plus several secondary wives or concubines, the number of a man's consorts reflecting his wealth, charm, and good health.

Shōnagon's journal was to give posterity a rare chronicle of life in Heian aristocratic circles, but like most court ladies, she only rarely encountered common people and treated them with haughty disdain. When she ran into a throng of commoners in a temple, she thought they "looked like so many basket-worms as they crowded together in their hideous clothes," alternately squatting and prostrating themselves. She was disgusted when uncouth lower-class women rushed to gather the leftovers after a palace banquet. But she confessed herself impressed by the skill of the peasants she saw harvesting a rice paddy, pulling the plants out by their roots and trimming off the ears.

Those peasants who tilled the fields, cleared the forests, built the palaces and temples, and fished the offshore waters were the only economically productive class in Japan. Everyone else lived off their labor. Yet they passed their toilsome days beneath the contemptuous gaze of Shōnagon and other writers of the time. The words that the aristocratic ladies ap-

In another court ceremony, dancers perform on a stage near the emperor's chamber *(far right)* to the tunes of two groups of musicians—men playing lutes, flutes, and percussion instruments *(lower left)*; and women in a separate compartment set off by banners *(upper left)*, performing on lute, zither, and chimes as two dancers rest nearby. This festival, which took place on January 20, was one of more than a dozen observances at court during that one month alone, including the Ceremony of the Blue Horses, in which twenty-one mounts from the imperial stables were paraded before the emperor; and the Bowmen's Wager, in which rival bands of imperial guards competed at archery, with the winners garnering prizes at a banquet.

Beneath cherry trees in full blossom, a group of aristocrats clad in colorful silks plays the ball game known as *kemari,* whose object was simply to keep the inflated leather sphere in the air as long as possible. On one occasion in the year 905, a court chronicle recorded, a gifted circle of players managed to pass the ball 260 times before it touched the ground.

plied to them—*esemono* and *esebito*—meant "doubtful creatures." They were regarded as barely human, incapable of the refinement and sensibility that marked "people of quality."

A passage in the great Japanese novel of this era, *The Tale of Genji,* written by another literary woman, Murasaki Shikibu, conveyed the perception of the peasantry as almost otherworldly beings. Murasaki, a high-born court lady, wrote: "The dawn was heralded by the raucous voices of peddlers crying their wares. The noises they made were entirely unintelligible. There seemed to be whole tribes of them. There was something ghostly about them as, seen against the gray morning sky, they struggled along with strange packages piled high upon their heads." The poet-statesman Michizane was perhaps the only writer who described the lot of the poor with compassion: "The aged who cannot afford meat must be cared for and comforted," he wrote. "The orphans who would otherwise starve and sleep without pillows must be aided." But neither Michizane nor anyone else did much to aid them.

By Heian times the distinction between slaves and free peasants that had existed earlier in Japan had eroded, and a single, large underclass of serfs made up the labor force. Most of them practiced subsistence farming on private shōen or on government land. Peasants were bound to their plots, but in lean years they would sometimes flee in search of a better livelihood elsewhere. Whenever desertions became widespread, however, officials would require that travelers carry identification—which, of course, was difficult to obtain.

The masses knew nothing but poverty and toil and the occasional relief offered by a Shinto festival or a wedding. Their huts were miserable wood-floored shanties, and their diets consisted almost entirely of rice; one edict, in fact, specifically forbade peasants to eat fish or drink wine. While Heian courtiers garbed themselves in silk and parried with poetry, the poor toiled in an obscurity so deep that the contemporary chroniclers barely noted their existence.

In the three centuries before the Heian era, the Japanese had imported much of their higher culture—their written language and literature, their educational system, their passion for calligraphy, and their artistic and architectural styles—directly from China. But from the eighth century on, a particularly Japanese culture with its own recognizable forms and conventions began to emerge.

To convert their spoken language to a written form, the Japanese first had to modify complex Chinese ideographs, in which the intricate patterns of lines represented ideas and things as well as sounds. Their solution was to abbreviate Chinese characters so that they became phonetic symbols without any other meaning. Each

A Touch with Paper

The art of papermaking reached an advanced state in the Heian age of Japan, as evidenced by these inscribed pages from a poetry anthology—collages of colored paper depicting scenes from nature, with details printed and painted on. The paper was produced using the time-honored technique devised in China: Vegetable pulp was strained through a rectangular sieve, leaving a fibrous layer behind on the mesh that formed a sheet when dried in the sun. Introduced to Japan in the seventh century, the process was soon being adapted there to yield colored sheets for collages such as the ones here or for the intimate poems that aristocratic couples exchanged. In springtime, for example, a young man might take out a green sheet of paper, inscribe it with love lyrics, and then send the note to his paramour along with an oak sprig in fresh leaf.

This 165-pound bronze phoenix was one of two crowning the so-called Phoenix Hall *(overleaf)*, a shrine at Uji dedicated to the Buddha Amida, who promised salvation to all who invoked his name. In Asia, the mythical bird—which died and rose again from the ashes of its own funeral pyre—was a sign of hope. The devotees of Amida may have regarded the phoenix as an emblem of the western paradise, or Pure Land, to which they aspired after death.

symbol corresponded to a syllable in the Japanese tongue. With these new symbols, the Japanese could write simply and clearly in the language they spoke.

Calligraphy was almost as important as poetry in Heian society. The skill and precision with which the brush strokes were applied in a poem or letter was seen as a sign of character and breeding and a mirror of the soul; more than merely a means of expression, it was an art form with moral overtones. Shōnagon's claim that she could assess an individual's worth from a single word was a judgment based on calligraphy. A character in Murasaki's *Tale of Genji*, spying the address on a note a girl has written to the hero, sees "a great depth of feeling in the penmanship" and concludes, "Small wonder that Genji felt about the girl as he did."

The Confucian code of education adopted by the Japanese mandated a major university in the capital and smaller colleges in each province. The main purpose of education was to prepare the sons of the nobility for posts in government. The imperial provincial colleges never flourished, primarily because of a shortage of teachers. But the university in Heian-kyō became a celebrated center of learning with an enrollment at times approaching 400. Students attended classes in history, literature, the Confucian classics, and law, and they adhered to a strict regimen: examinations every tenth day, sharp discipline, and prompt dismissal of those who proved unable to measure up.

Students aspired to pass one of five civil service examinations. The highest exam cut across all disciplines and required a combination of great knowledge and high reasoning ability; success, rarely achieved, conferred an accolade of "exceptional talent." The other examinations, in descending order of importance, corresponded to courses of study: learning in the classics, knowledge of the principles of government, legal matters, and the ability to calculate.

In theory, the sons of commoners could attend the university, but in practice almost none did. In 914, a courageous scholar named Miyoshi Kiyotsura petitioned the emperor Daigo to reform the rampant favoritism accorded the upper classes. "Professors do not take into account the talent of the candidates, but simply glance at the names," he wrote. His plea apparently had little effect, and in time, the quality of education at the university declined to the point where the great families established their own private schools. Eventually, the once-great university at Heian-kyō was virtually abandoned, the classrooms all but empty, and the grounds overgrown with weeds.

In architecture, the Heian style was subdued understatement with an emphasis on allowing structures to blend in harmoniously with their natural settings. The mansions of the nobles, called *shinden,* were one-story, rectangular wooden structures with thatched roofs. A typical compound held several simple buildings connected by covered passageways and surrounded by a low white wall. A main house giving on to a garden was flanked by the residences of the owner's principal wife, his consorts, and other family members. Each house was essentially a single large room with movable partitions that could be used to section it as occasion demanded. Carved gates, their height and decorations attesting to the householder's rank, punctuated the outside wall on three sides.

The real glory of a Heian-kyō manor was its elaborate landscaped garden, with miniature ponds and streams and islands, the whole set with ornamental rocks. The garden was the setting for most ceremonies and entertainments, and removable shutters and blinds on the side of the house facing the garden permitted an indoor-outdoor effect. Some shinden gardens boasted miniature reproductions of Japan's scenic marvels; one re-created a famous bay in the north filled with hundreds of pine-forested islands.

In art, Heian painters expanded their repertoire beyond religious themes to include nature and court life, especially in the illustrated scrolls called *emakimono* that related a story in a series of illustrations. Often attached to screens or sliding doors, emakimono depicted historical events as well as landscapes peopled by contemporary courtiers. Japanese artists were sensitive to natural vistas and the changes of seasons—a gentle summer rain or a meadow bursting with spring blossoms.

Religious art focused on statues of Buddhist or Shinto figures, but now carved from wood, rather than the bronze or clay favored by earlier Japanese sculptors. Like the Chinese, the Japanese enjoyed transforming everyday objects into objects of art: Mirrors, inkstands, writing brushes, go boards, and wooden boxes were often lacquered or inlaid with mother-of-pearl.

But it was literature—poetry and prose—that best exemplified the Heian creative spirit. The popularity of Chinese verses waned during the ninth century, and at the urging of Emperor Uda, the first anthologies of poems in Japanese forms began to appear. A list of the subjects treated in one collection shows the range of topics deemed appropriate for poetry: banquets, history, tender farewells, grief, music, religion, sad regrets, love, sending and receiving gifts. The preferred form was the five-line *waka: This perfectly still / Spring day bathed in the soft light / From the spread-out sky / Why do the cherry blossoms / So restlessly scatter down?*

A master such as Michizane, who composed in many styles, Japanese as well as Chinese, could write of a personal sorrow—the death of a son—with a poignant artistry that transcended time and language:

> How can I bear to hear your sisters call your name, searching;
> To see your mother waste away her life in grief . . .
> Your mulberry bow over the door, the mugwort arrows;
> Your stilts by the hedge top, the riding whip of vine;
> In the garden the flower seeds we planted in fun;
> On the wall, words you'd learned, your scribblings beside them—
> Each time I recall your voice, your laugh, you are here again.

Murasaki Shikibu, the eleventh-century author who wrote *The Tale of Genji*, was, like Sei Shōnagon, a lady-in-waiting to an empress. A member of a minor branch of the Fujiwara family known for its cultivation and literary skill, she was as shy as Shōnagon was saucy. Murasaki, in fact, regarded Shōnagon as "frivolous" and remarked on her "extraordinary air of self-satisfaction."

Both women wrote in Japanese because Chinese, which was still viewed as the language of the learned during their lifetime, was thought to be too difficult for women. It was thus left to them, and especially Murasaki, to produce the finest prose of the Heian age and the first great writing in Japanese. The 630,000-word *Tale of Genji* would later be counted by some scholars as both the world's first novel in any

THE HALL OF PARADISE

Erected on the west bank of the Uji River, the Phoenix Hall was dedicated by Fujiwara no Yorimichi, son of the powerful statesman Michinaga, in the year 1052. The date was a fateful one, for according to Buddhist lore the apocalyptic age known as *Mappō*, or the End of the Law, had just begun. Convinced that the world was descending into anarchy, followers of the Buddha Amida looked to the next life, and the Phoenix Hall afforded them a preview of that goal. Pilgrims approaching the shrine could glimpse the Buddha's serene face through a screen at the main entrance. And the very structure of the hall mimicked the auspicious form of the phoenix, with two graceful wings and a long tail section trailing behind.

language and the supreme classic of Japanese literature. In the book, a finely crafted episodic chronicle, Murasaki traced the fortunes of more than 400 characters over three-quarters of a century. Its hero Hikaru Genji—the name means "the shining prince"—was born the son of an emperor and one of his lesser concubines. Genji was a paragon of the virtues most admired by Heian Japanese women—a man of taste and refinement, a talented poet and musician, and a virtuoso lover, forever searching for the ideal woman. His odyssey became a study of triumphs, follies, and anguish, of the subtle interplay of human relations. At one point, trying to share his hard-won experience with his son, Genji advised the boy that "we tend to be attracted precisely by those people with whom it is most impossible that we should be permanently connected." Genji knows: He has sired an illegitimate child by one of his father's consorts. The story moved from the palaces and shinden of Heian-kyō to rural monasteries and peasant huts, and was always alive with evocations of nature and the seasons: "The wisteria and mountain-kerria were in full bloom, loveliest of all at evening, when the setting sun slanted through the hanging sprays of delicate blossom. This was a moment of the year that had always given him an intense delight." But Genji and his son Kaoru learned that melancholy is often the handmaiden of beauty. The book exemplified the Heian aesthetic called *mono no aware* —the capacity to be moved, a recognition that sadness shadows all lives. When his wife died, Genji asked himself "what use they had ever been—this beauty, these talents that were supposed to raise him above all his peers? No sooner did he come into the world than loneliness and sorrow fell to his share."

Genji's discovery of the sad and fleeting nature of life echoed Japanese religious thought during the Heian years. It was an eclectic blend of traditional Buddhism represented by various sects, Chinese yin-yang dualism, and the ancient Shinto beliefs. The Japanese adopted ideas from all of them in the conduct of both government and daily life. The surface contradictions—between the Buddhist rejection of transitory pleasure, for example, and Shinto's joyous embrace of the natural world—were muted and fused into a single, all-inclusive religion. Adherence to one set of beliefs did not demand the rejection of another.

The two principal Buddhist sects were established by a pair of ninth-century monks who found their inspiration in China, Saichō and Kūkai. Both traveled to the Middle Kingdom in 804 to study Chinese Buddhism. Saichō returned to set up the Tendai sect, which preached the supremacy of the universal Buddha and declared that salvation could be attained through meditation, good works, virtuous conduct, and reading the Lotus Sutra scripture.

Tendai priests, ensconced at their sprawling headquarters—which eventually numbered 3,000 buildings—on Mount Hiei northeast of Heian-kyō, led the way in syn-

The bodhisattva above, perched on wispy clouds and tapping a drum held in a lotus cup, was one of fifty-two angelic music makers that greeted worshipers as they entered the main chamber of the Phoenix Hall. At the western end of the sanctuary, between the carved-wood bodhisattvas, sat the gilded image of the Buddha Amida on his lotus throne *(opposite)*. For a follower, to stand before that throne was to anticipate the triumph of one's dying moment, when the Amida would descend to earth with his host of attendants to carry the soul away to the Pure Land.

thesizing the religious ideas current in Japan into one creed. Tendai became the most powerful Buddhist group in Japan, partly because of its tolerance of diversity, and it eventually embraced popular forms that spread Buddhism to the common folk.

Kūkai, the other voyaging monk, was a many-sided genius celebrated as one of the great men in Japanese history. He was a poet and scholar, a painter, and the finest calligrapher of his time as well as a renowned teacher. Kūkai's Shingon sect, derived

from another faction of Chinese Buddhism, was known as the True Word. Less theoretical than Tendai, Shingon shared its acceptance of the universal Buddha but differed on the route to salvation. This state of bliss could be achieved only through knowledge of the true word, which the leader of the sect passed on to but one chosen disciple on his deathbed.

Shingon stressed incantations and secret rituals centering on "the three mysteries" of the mind, speech, and body. A believer practiced the speech mystery by chanting *mantras* and expressed the mystery of the body in hand motions called *mudras*. The Shingon faithful meditated with the aid of cosmic diagrams known as *mandalas,* often artfully executed as scroll paintings and carvings. Shingon's esoteric and exclusive elements made it popular with the aristocrats at the Heian court.

Buddhist ideas permeated Heian culture and affected everyday life: The Buddhist practice of cremation began to replace burials, meat eating was proscribed, and banishment often supplanted the death penalty as the ultimate punishment. But the doctrinal intricacies of Buddhism meant little to the ordinary Japanese until the emergence in the tenth century of the cult that revolved around the "pure land" Buddha Amida. He was the Buddha who had promised salvation to sentient beings, and the pure land was a paradise in the hereafter accessible to anyone who professed faith in Amida and invoked his name in a special prayer. This simple creed, with its promise of easy salvation, rapidly became the most popular form of Buddhism among all classes of Japanese society.

The yin-yang cosmology that had originated in China, with its division of nature into two halves—the yin of earth, water, darkness, and women, and the yang of fire, light, action, and men—was incorporated into Heian government. Experts in the Bureau of Divination were called upon to identify the yin-yang implications of state policies. They reported to the council of state on the good and bad omens, astrological factors, and directional taboos that were relevant to government decisions.

Buddhist doctrine was able to absorb the simple Shinto beliefs by accepting Shinto deities as manifestations of the Buddhas. The great Buddha Dainichi was identified with the Shinto sun goddess, Amaterasu, the cult's supreme being. Yet the shrine of the goddess remained the holiest place in Japan, and a place from which Buddhist elements were excluded. Even Heian courtiers accepted the Shinto notions that death, childbirth, and illness were visitations of uncleanliness that made a house taboo. Wooden tags on the homes of the afflicted warned visitors to stay away.

Even highly educated Japanese adhered to hundreds of superstitious beliefs derived from Shintoism. Vengeful gods and the spirits of the dead could possess people or place curses on them. Directions were always significant. Northeast was permanently unlucky, while others were inauspicious at particular times in a person's life. Northwest could be dangerous for a sixteen-year-old, for example. Dreams and strange natural phenomena were charged with meaning: When a peculiar smoky mist appeared over Heian-kyō, the masters concluded that it foreshadowed a typhoon, flood, or fire. (In actuality, on one such occasion an earthquake occurred shortly thereafter.) On the "night of the monkey," which came around once every sixty days, people had to leave home and stay awake all night to protect themselves from the evil "corpse worms" that attacked sleeping bodies.

Sneezing was ominous—when the empress Sadako heard someone sneeze she said, "Oh dear, so you're telling a lie." Sorcerers could render themselves invisible by donning a straw cloak, and people who fell asleep wearing their clothes inside out would have pleasant dreams. Exorcists attempted to cure the ill through incantations that supposedly transferred the malevolent spirit causing the disease from the sick person to a medium. Shōnagon described an exorcism, which she declared a success—"the priest brought the spirit under control, and having forced it to beg for mercy, dismissed it."

In one of the homilies Heian aristocrats were forever writing for their heirs, a tenth-century Fujiwara noble named Morosuke offered precise guidance on how to get through a day with minimal risk: "First repeat seven times in a low voice the name of the star for the year. Then look at the calendar and see whether the day is one of good or evil omen. Cut your fingernails on a day of the ox, your toenails on a day of the tiger. If the day is auspicious, now bathe, but only once every fifth day. Early in life select a divinity as the object of your devotion and chant his holy name, after cleansing your hands in a basin of water."

The early Heian years were marked by harmony and accommodation between different Japanese religious institutions. Later, this tolerance gave way to sectarian strife motivated by greed as well as by doctrinal differences, causing religious upheavals that hastened the end of Heian society. Despite all efforts to restrict their temporal power, the monasteries became landowners on a par with the great noble families. As early as 850, the Tōdaiji monastery near Nara owned 30,000 acres of arable land, nearly one percent of all the land under cultivation in Japan. And the monasteries jealously guarded their domains both from imperial interference and from each other. When the Tendai sect split into two factions in the late tenth century, the opposing groups recruited gangs of peasant guards—called akusō, or "bad monks"—which eventually evolved into formidable armies.

The mercenaries hired by Buddhist monasteries and Shinto shrines first concen-

As Heian civilization declined, grim visions flourished in Buddhist art along with soothing images of paradise. Here, hungry ghosts rummage through a cemetery to pick at the bones of the dead in a scene from a twelfth-century Buddhist scroll detailing the fate of greedy souls caught in limbo. Such depictions reminded those who were still reluctant to renounce their earthly appetites of the plight that awaited them beyond the grave—a ghostly life of unslaked craving. Though promulgated by monks, this eerie view of the afterlife owed part of its appeal to Japanese folklore, which held that those unfortunates who died with troubled spirits would return to haunt the world.

In another Buddhist scroll painting of the late Heian period, a demon crushes thieves and other reprobates beneath an iron mortar as a subaltern carries off the bones of previous victims

a tray *(right)*. Unlike the ghosts on page 123, who could still be saved by the Buddha, the sinners in this infernal zone—one of 128 cited in Buddhist texts—lie beyond redemption.

trated on attacking and looting their rivals' headquarters. In 1081, the Kōfukuji monks of Nara joined with another monastery to attack two enemy monasteries, pillaging one and burning the other to the ground. Some years later, those same Nara monks sent a force of 20,000 men against the Enryakuji monks on Mount Hiei near the capital. The fighting often had nothing to do with sacred issues but was a matter of pure lust for land and power.

The monks then turned to intimidating the imperial government in order to gain court positions or land grants. Warrior monks from Mount Hiei swooped into Heian-kyō time after time between 981 and 1185, laying siege to the palace and ministers' homes to press their demands. Since the imperial court lacked a standing army, it was often forced to capitulate. Even so, the invaders burned parts of the lovely city, and large sections became the haunt of robbers and outlaws. One eleventh-century emperor observed that the three things beyond his control were the floods of the Kamo River, the perils of gambling, and the Mount Hiei monks.

The emperor was in fact giving himself more credit than he deserved, because by the eleventh century most of Japan was utterly beyond his control. The political and economic power of the regime had declined steadily as the tax-free provincial estates owned both by powerful noble families and by Buddhist monasteries increased in size, wealth, and influence. The provincial warlords were made from a different mold than the Heian courtiers; rugged and self-sufficient, they ruled their fiefdoms with private armies and defied the government whenever they wished. Aristocrats on horseback, they were the Japanese equivalent of the barons of medieval Europe.

This cryptic sketch, credited to a twelfth-century monk, uses animal figures to shed a satiric light on human affairs in Japan. At left, a motley crowd of spectators, including a bonneted monkey and a hooded fox, look on with an air of wry indulgence as two frogs perform a humble folk dance; another frog at center, wearing a court cap like his feline companion, appears to find the spectacle less enchanting. At right, foxes, hares, and frogs surround a wounded frog, their mouths agape—a sign of surprise, perhaps, or cruel amusement. Although the precise intentions of the artist remain obscure, the sketch seems to reflect the jaundiced view of society that took hold among monks and scholars as the Heian court lost authority in Japan and turmoil increased.

The warrior clans formed alliances based on marriage and friendship and fought a series of small wars among themselves, interrupted by periodic calls from the capital to mount a show of force in behalf of one faction or another during the time of the cloistered emperors. When a bitter succession dispute between ex-emperors Toba and Sutoku (who were father and son) arose in 1155, Toba's faction owed its victory to the support of the two clans that had by then established themselves as preeminent, the Minamoto and the Taira.

In the ensuing thirty years these two families, both claiming descent from the imperial line, vied for the supremacy that had once been the exclusive prerogative of the Fujiwara. It was a contest that would usher in the age of feudal *shoguns* while signaling the doom of the Heian era of peace and tranquillity. The Taira won the first test of strength, and their leader installed himself as prime minister, adopting the Fujiwara custom of marrying his daughter to the emperor and then elevating their son—his grandson—to the throne.

The Minamoto withdrew to their stronghold in the Kantō plain near present-day Tokyo and bided their time. In 1180, they launched an all-out campaign that lasted five years and resulted in the total annihilation of the Taira. The Taira emperor died with his relatives in the concluding battle of the war. The leader of the triumphant clan, Minamoto Yoritomo, permitted the emperor's successor to retain the throne and the palace in Heian-kyō while he ran the government from a seaside town in the provinces—the hinterlands that the now-powerless Heian courtiers had long disdained. The era of the cloud-dwellers was at an end.

MONUMENT BUILDERS IN THE AMERICAS

4 Time and again it happened, at isolated points across the vast sweep of the American hemisphere. A tribal people, grown prosperous through trade or agriculture, began to build on a colossal scale. At the opening of the ninth century, signs of this phenomenon—both from the past and currently in progress—were visible at a number of sites in the Americas. In Mexico's central valley, the huge, stone pyramids of Teotihuacán, though recently abandoned, continued to inspire awe. The ornate temple towers of the Maya still lifted majestically over the Guatemalan rain forest, and handsome new Mayan complexes had begun to rise in the grassy, sun-drenched hills of Yucatan. Thousands of miles to the south, from a great stone capital in the Andes Mountains, the royal acolytes of a mysterious, staff-bearing god held far-reaching power, much like their Chavín forebears who had constructed huge temple complexes of their own more than a millennium earlier. And now the urge to build was asserting itself in yet another American region.

After centuries of simple society, the peoples inhabiting the lands that eventually would become the United States were building on a grand scale. In both the southwestern deserts and the woodlands of the east, North Americans were erecting shrines, fortresses, even prototype cities, some of great size and sophistication.

The main focus of this construction activity in the eastern part of North America was the broad, fertile valley of the great river later named the Mississippi, which drained the center of the continent. Some time around AD 800, in an area dotted by thatch-roofed villages and hunting camps, organized battalions of laborers set to work creating a number of imposing tribal capitals. The chief building material was packed earth—baskets of soil heaped into immense rectangular piles and firmly tamped into place. It seemed as though the architects were attempting to rival the mountain-building forces of nature itself. Great pyramid-like platforms, some nearing 100 feet in height and covering several acres, rose up to flank broad ceremonial plazas. Processional staircases buttressed with logs swept up the platforms' sides, past wide earth terraces, to wooden temples or noblemen's residences atop the mounds. Palisade walls, constructed of stout wooden pilings jammed tightly together and complete with projecting strongpoints, or bastions, surrounded the inner precincts as a barrier against attack. Below, lapping at the platforms' bases like waves against a headland, crowded the huts of commoners.

Scores of these fortified centers rose along the length of the Mississippi and its tributaries, from the Great Lakes to the Gulf of Mexico. They sprang up as far afield as the eastern edge of the Great Plains, deep in the Appalachian Mountains, and in the lake country of the Florida panhandle. Some, over the centuries, would develop from towns into cities with thousands of inhabitants.

In fact, these were not the first such structures in the region. The landscape was

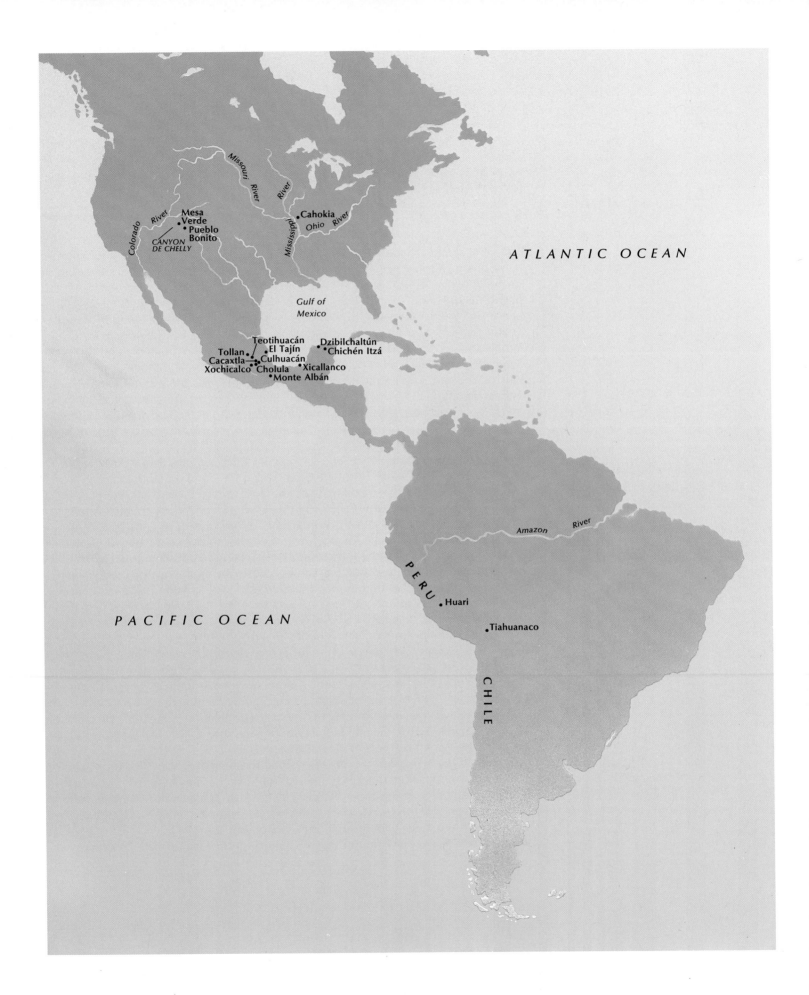

ATLANTIC OCEAN

PACIFIC OCEAN

Colorado River

Missouri River

River

Mesa Verde

Pueblo Bonito

CANYON DE CHELLY

Cahokia

Ohio River

Mississippi

Gulf of Mexico

Teotihuacán

Tollan

El Tajín

Dzibilchaltún

Chichén Itzá

Cacaxtla

Culhuacán

Xochicalco

Cholula

Xicallanco

Monte Albán

Amazon River

PERU

Huari

Tiahuanaco

CHILE

already patterned with long-abandoned earthworks built by peoples who had resided in eastern North America many centuries earlier. By 1000 BC, the inhabitants of the region lived in scattered single-family homesteads, stalking deer, bear, and small game in the forest, fishing the rivers, and foraging for seeds, nuts, berries, acorns, and other wild plant foods. Many tribes also tended small plots where they cultivated a number of domesticated plants, including squash, gourds, sunflowers, marsh elder, and lamb's-quarters. They fashioned tools from stone, wood, and bone, and some groups made a utilitarian pottery by hand-coiling rolled strings of clay into crude vessels. Then around 600 BC, a people known to future archaeologists as the Adena—from the site of one of their ritual centers in the Ohio Valley—took a long step forward. They began to bury the bodies of their most prominent persons in graves marked by commemorative earthen mounds.

The Adena exhibited great ingenuity in constructing these mounds. They were generally arranged in clusters within ceremonial enclosures—neat truncated cones and hummocks up to around twenty feet in height, surrounded by low earthen ramparts in the shape of circles, squares, pentagons, or other geometric forms. The Adena added new graves to existing mounds over the years, so the mounds grew.

The burials became increasingly elaborate as time went on, and status distinctions began to appear. Tribal leaders were laid out in sturdy, log-lined tombs. Their bodies were sprinkled with red ocher or graphite, and they were accompanied by appropriate tools and ornaments to ensure their successful entrance into the afterlife. Occasionally a polished skull, perhaps a war trophy, was included. Individuals of lesser rank were commonly cremated, and their ashes interred.

Fully as much effort went into fashioning grave ornaments as into building the mounds themselves. Adena artisans carved slate tablets with stylized insignia and cut animal silhouettes from sheets of mica, thin leaves of crystalline rock acquired in trade from the area that later would be North Carolina. A favored motif was a bird of prey with hooked beak and needle-sharp talons. Copper nuggets, obtained by trade with tribes around the Great Lakes, took on ceremonial glitter as bracelets, spiral-shaped rings, spool-like neck ornaments, and ritual axheads. Important individuals were sometimes buried with ceremonial pipes—tubes of polished stone occasionally carved to resemble a human figure. No botanical evidence would survive to indicate that the Adena had tobacco, which possibly did not appear in eastern North America until centuries later. Perhaps they smoked some other leafy plant.

A few Adena earthworks differed from the geometric burial mounds, and these would be a source of endless speculation to scholars of later eras. One striking example was a huge earthen snake that twined across a ridge in southwest Ohio. No graves or artifacts would be found in the Great Serpent Mound. It apparently was constructed in late Adena times purely as a monumental act of faith. It was enormous, measuring along the sinuous curves of its length nearly a quarter of a mile from tip to tail. Its mouth gaped wide to gobble down an earthen oval: a primordial egg? the sun? a departed soul? The builders left no clue.

Around 200 BC, the Adena were succeeded in the Ohio Valley by an even more dedicated group of mound builders, who showed even greater talents as architects and artisans. Later known as the Hopewell, from one of their ceremonial sites, they carried Adena cultural traditions to a new, higher level of sophistication. Their cemetery compounds were of immense scale, with open plazas hundreds of yards across and processional avenues leading several miles into the countryside.

The regions inhabited by the dozen and more advanced American cultures that flourished during the first millennium AD described a huge S-curve through the continents. The Mississippi watershed was home to a succession of North American peoples: the Adena, Hopewell, and finally, Mississippian, whose principal city was Cahokia. In the valleys and canyons of the American southwest lived three notably inventive cultures—the Anasazi, Hohokam, and Mogollon. Mexico and Central America saw a dazzling succession of civilizations—Maya, Mixtec, Zapotec, Toltec—that established impressive cities such as Tollan and Dzibilchaltún. Other accomplished builders were the inhabitants of the South American Andean highlands with their monumental city of Tiahuanaco, perched 12,500 feet high, and another great metropolis, Huari, that housed 75,000 people.

Hundreds of Hopewellian mound centers were constructed, not only in the Ohio Valley but also in other areas throughout the east. Perhaps restless groups of Hopewell people ventured into new territories, carrying their culture with them. More likely, the centers were built by different peoples, widely separated by geography, who through long-distance trade exchanged ideas as well as goods and developed similar interests in the construction of burial mounds and geometric earthworks.

Whether or not the builders were related, they conducted a lively commerce in exotic raw materials and finished artifacts, items which frequently ended up as luxurious grave offerings. A conch shell from the Gulf Coast, a grizzly bear tooth from the Rocky Mountains—these were highly prized items to be fashioned into ornaments for the wardrobe of a tribal leader living, say, along the middle reaches of the Mississippi River, and upon his death they would be laid beside him in his burial mound.

Perhaps trading parties from the Hopewell villages would set out along the rivers in small convoys of dugout canoes, each laden with articles of local manufacture to be exchanged for goods and materials produced by other tribes. Most voyages were probably short, seldom lasting more than a week or two. The usual destination was a riverside trading post where tribes from the surrounding territories would meet periodically, perhaps at the same time every year, to barter and feast. Some would bring objects from distant regions to be exchanged for a second or third time. By this means goods would travel from tribe to tribe within far-reaching, interlocking networks of mainly waterborne commerce. At the same time, Hopewell customs spread out along the trade routes, to influence distant tribes whose languages and cultures were totally different.

The Hopewell trade network covered a vast expanse of territory, reaching out to include most of the continent east of the Rocky Mountains. Obsidian from Yellowstone found its way into south-central Ohio to be shaped into arrowheads, knives, and other cutting tools. Silver came in from Ontario, copper from Lake Superior, chalcedony from North Dakota, mica and quartz crystals from the Appalachians. From Florida and the Gulf came a cornucopia of exotic goods, including turtle shells, whelks, shark teeth, barracuda jaws, and alligator skulls.

A major Ohio export item was a prized variety of flintlike chert, ideal for making tools and weapons. Almost as important was a fine-grained stone much favored by pipe carvers. Hopewell pipes were objects of consummate artistry, far surpassing the early Adena efforts. The usual design was a sculpted animal perched on a rectangular base. Beavers, bears, panthers, hawks, owls, geese, ravens—almost the entire bestiary of forest life was represented. A cavity scooped out of the creature's back or head formed the bowl, while a drilled hole transformed the base into a flattened pipestem. The carvers depicted their subjects with a marvelous realism, carefully outlining the

This gleaming, undulating snake, cut from a single, thin sheet of mica, was made by a Hopewell artisan for burial with a dead chief or noble. The Hopewell, who flourished in the Ohio River basin until AD 600, ranged widely, trading with other peoples for minerals, shells, and other objects from which to fashion ornaments and ceremonial images. The mica used for this snake probably came from the Appalachian Mountains, several hundred miles away.

feathers of an eagle or the markings on a toad's mottled skin, and sometimes indicating eyes and teeth with inlaid bone or freshwater pearl.

Hopewell artisans also worked in hand-coiled clay, creating fired pots and figurines of considerable elegance. Ceramic bowls with textured designs, some recalling the Adena bird of prey motif, made treasured grave offerings. So did the figurines, which often showed dignified young women in the casual attitudes of daily life. Here a maiden sat primly on the ground, there a young mother nursed her baby or carried an older child piggyback.

For all the majesty of their ceremonial sites, neither the Adena nor the Hopewell lived much differently from their ancestors. Adena families dwelled in large circular houses of woven sticks, with log posts supporting a roof of grass or branches. Smoke from the hearth wafted upward through a hole in the roof. Perhaps half a dozen such dwellings would occupy a clearing in the Ohio forest—seldom more. Agriculture remained at a primitive level, with villagers cultivating small fields.

The Hopewell were better farmers. They mastered the rudiments of cultivating a variety of indigenous crops. But they, too, sustained themselves primarily by hunting and gathering. And although the Hopewell sometimes clustered together in slightly larger groups than the Adena, often in the river bottoms below the ceremonial centers, their scattered settlements usually contained only one or two thatch-roofed houses occupied by a few families.

Neither the Adena nor the Hopewell would leave behind any indication of how such small societies could get enough people together and work to a single plan to create their mounds. Scholars of the future, finding no evidence of any sizable organization, would be baffled about what kind of individual or group imposed the unity of direction that made those architectural achievements possible.

Even so, over time the Hopewell burial rites grew ever more lavish, their ceremonial compounds larger and more elaborate. Then, around AD 400, the energies of the mound builders began to wane. Perhaps a subtle shift in climate affected their food supply; perhaps the bonds of treaty and common purpose that tied together the trade network began to fray. For whatever reason, the funeral offerings declined in quality, and by AD 500, no new burial compounds were being constructed. On the northern fringe areas of Hopewell territory (the lands that later would become Iowa, Minnesota, and Wisconsin), some Hopewellian groups continued to raise effigy earthworks in the spirit of the Adena's Great Serpent. Gargantuan birds, bears, panthers, and human figures sprawled out across the countryside. But in the midcontinental core of the Ohio Valley, and across most of the east, mound construction virtually ceased.

The ninth century, however, saw a new era of mound building get under way. Once again great earthen pyramids rose above the woodland riverbanks—and on a more ambitious scale than ever before. Mounds soon appeared throughout the entire sweep of the continent's central watershed, from the Great Lakes to the Gulf of Mexico, and across the Appalachians to

A tiny, vivid effigy of a beaver, with eyes of freshwater pearl and teeth made of bone inlay, forms part of a pipe used in Hopewell religious ceremonies. The pipe's bowl was a cavity in the beaver's back; smoke was drawn through the hole visible in the near end. The pipe was found in western Illinois, about 350 miles from the Hopewell heartland. Hopewell influence spread even farther—west onto the Great Plains, south to the Gulf of Mexico, and north into the area that later would be called Minnesota.

the Atlantic seaboard. Because so much of the construction was centered about the Mississippi River, the people responsible would later be known as Mississippians.

The Mississippi builders ushered in a new spirit of vitality and material progress, far outstripping their Hopewell predecessors. They raised their earthworks not exclusively as cemeteries to honor the dead, but as monuments to celebrate the living. Built to larger proportions than ever before, the mounds occupied broad plazas at the center of bustling tribal communities. Here they served as platforms for fine private houses and civic and religious buildings—meeting lodges and temples dedicated to their tribal ancestors.

The new boom in construction was pushed along by improving skills, not all of them directly involving building techniques. One important development was a breakthrough in agriculture. The Hopewell had cultivated the maize that Americans would later call corn, but until this era it had remained a minor crop, just one plant food among a variety on which people depended. Sometime between AD 800 and 1000, however, corn became the primary staple, the basic stuff of life and the most important crop that the inhabitants of eastern North America grew. Looking back on this development from the modern period, some scholars would speculate that the change resulted from the introduction of a new strain of cold-resistant, high-yielding corn brought north by traders from Mexico. (And some would suggest that the same traders also inspired local inhabitants with accounts of Middle American pyramid construction, thus setting off the new mound-building boom.) But the Mississippians would leave no evidence that such was the case or that they participated in any commerce with Mexico, and the rise of corn-based agriculture may well have been impelled by other causes. In any case, the result was a widespread burst of prosperity and an increase in population. In the days of hunting, foraging, and casual farming, the land could support perhaps one person per square mile. Now, with intensive corn farming, five times as many people could thrive in the same space.

Newly prosperous through agriculture, the Mississippians congregated in villages larger than the hamlets of their predecessors, some populous enough to be called towns. Each town had its ceremonial center of earthen platforms and was probably ruled by a high-ranking group of individuals, perhaps elite warriors. One of the largest centers was Cahokia, on the east bank of the Mississippi in what would become Illinois. Cahokia's earliest settlers had arrived around AD 600 to farm the area's fertile bottomlands. The site, near the confluence of the Mississippi and Ohio rivers, was well placed for trade along those waterways and was close to several sources of important raw materials, including a large flint quarry a short journey downriver.

As Cahokia prospered and expanded, it began to assume a commanding position over the surrounding communities. The size of its granaries and the vitality of its traders undoubtedly played a major role. But in all likelihood, a certain degree of force was also brought to bear. The supply of good farmland was limited; only the soft, loamy bottomlands along the rivers yielded easily to cultivation by digging stick and flint-headed hoe, and were annually enriched by flood waters. The competition for prime acreage became heated as populations rose. And so, as their numbers increased, the Cahokians strained at the limits of their home territory and began expanding at the expense of their neighbors.

They made use of a relatively recent fundamental innovation in weaponry, the bow and arrow. For millennia, American hunters and warriors had relied mainly on stone-pointed spears hurled by hand or with the aid of a throwing stick known as an

A huge fifteen-acre temple mound *(upper right)* resembling the pyramids of Mexico and Central America dominated Cahokia, the principal city of the Mississippians, situated where East St. Louis, Illinois, would stand later. Around the religious shrine stretched clusters of workshops, dwellings, and farms, as well as other mounds, including the rectangular one in the foreground, a platform for human sacrifice, and the conical one next to it, used for burials. Beyond the protective walls more farms stretched across the rich bottomland of the Mississippi Valley. The largest city built north of Mexico during that era, Cahokia housed about 10,000 people during its heyday from AD 900 to 1100.

atlatl, which could greatly increase the spear's range. But sometime between the decline of the Hopewell and the rise of the Mississippians, someone discovered that a pliable tree branch, bowed and strung with some kind of tough plant fiber, could propel a flint-tipped arrow with deadly accuracy three times as far as a spear could be thrown. From then on, raids and ripostes between various groups left the Mississippi landscape littered with arrowheads.

However they asserted their power, the Cahokians raised their community to regional supremacy. And beginning around 900 they set about endowing it with appropriate pomp and majesty. The centerpiece was an enormous, multitiered earthen platform set in a ceremonial complex overlooking a side channel of the Mississippi. Built in stages over several centuries, it eventually encompassed almost nineteen acres. With a base that was 1,037 feet long and 790 feet wide, rising to a height of 100 feet, it was the third largest structure in the Americas at that time, exceeded only by two roughly similar temple pyramids in Mexico. More than 100 lesser mounds and platforms radiated out from the hub of the great monument, forming a ceremonial complex about five miles square. Some of these works formed the bases of shrines and temples, some the foundations of wooden residences for aristocratic warriors and administrators. Others marked family graves.

A stout, wooden stockade enclosed much of Cahokia's center, and beyond the walls, residential suburbs of thatch-walled common dwellings stretched for a dozen miles along both sides of the river. Year after year, the number of houses increased. By the time Cahokia reached its zenith in the eleventh century, the broadly dispersed settlement would be home to perhaps as many as 10,000 people—the largest concentration of population in America north of Mexico.

Only a powerful, central authority could have governed so large a population and mobilized it into erecting such edifices. Like most Mississippian centers, Cahokia probably was organized into a rigid hierarchical system. And although neither legend nor document would survive to describe this hierarchy—the Mississippians could not write, nor did they enjoy a strong oral tradition—one possible pocket of Mississippian culture would still exist centuries later when Europeans first arrived in the area. Eighteenth-century European accounts of that probably vestigial society, the Natchez tribe of Mississippi, would provide a glimpse into earlier Mississippian life.

The Fatherland site, near where the city named Natchez would one day stand, was the ceremonial center of the Natchez. It was here that their ruler, known as the Great Sun, resided in a house atop a mound, facing the main temple. Commoners lived in seven villages scattered through the nearby countryside. The Great Sun held his subjects in absolute thrall, with powers of life and death over everyone. His foot never touched the bare earth; servants carried him everywhere. Even his relatives, the Lesser Suns, crawled before him, although they filled the upper ranks of priests and warriors. Below them came the Nobles, followed by a class of Honored Men, which might include war heroes, master artisans, and traders. The bottom stratum was peopled by commoners and slaves, who did most of the real work. Low-ranking men or women who married above their class could thus boost their children to a higher status but would not themselves be elevated. Or a particularly ambitious individual might win special treatment by offering a close relative—a wife or son or daughter— for the state ritual of human sacrifice.

When the Great Sun himself died, he took to the grave all his wives and concubines, along with a few close male advisers and servants. So, apparently, did some of the higher nobles: In one burial site, a tribal lord was laid to rest accompanied by fifty-three freshly strangled women and six male retainers.

The Mississippian predecessors of the Natchez apparently were much attracted by ritual and ceremony of all kinds. Some tribes divided their members into two groups, one in charge of such key annual events as harvest festivals, the other responsible for organizing war dances and raiding parties. Preparations were plotted out in the men's lodge, a large, round, mud-plastered building with an adjoining courtyard in the city's main plaza. The lodge served as both meetinghouse and informal club, where tribal males might retire to smoke their pipes and confer with friends. No women were allowed over the threshold.

Another all-male occupation was the ancient game of chungke, part of the regional culture since Adena times. Two contestants, running abreast, would hurl eight-foot wooden poles at a stone disk that was bowled ahead of them down a court. The player whose pole landed closest to where the disk stopped rolling scored a point. An actual hit was worth two points.

Mississippi culture would not reach its zenith until the eleventh century, and it would flourish unchallenged for the next several hundred years. The decline, when it came, would occur first in the central Mississippi heartland, in Cahokia and its surrounding territory—the combined result, most likely, of overpopulation, disease, incessant warfare, and rising water tables that made much farmland too wet to cultivate. But the influence of this vital and far-reaching culture continued to be felt in outlying regions until the arrival of a new civilization from Europe—more than 800 years after the Mississippians first appeared.

Even before the Mississippian culture arose in eastern North America, a civilizing impulse, apparently from Middle America, had swept into the alkali flats and mesa lands to the southwest, where it blended with the age-old traditions of indigenous tribes. In this sere landscape, the inhabitants achieved a way of life that was a remarkable, peaceable accommodation, with nature and with each other.

Three principal groups occupied the region: the Hohokam, in what would become southern Arizona; the Mogollon, inhabitants of the mountains of what later would be New Mexico; and the Anasazi, who lived in the canyons and mesas of the vast Colorado Plateau. By all evidence these peoples existed side by side in near total harmony. No one marched into battle to gain land or prestige or scalps. No sharp distinctions of class seem to have separated ruler from ruled. There were no Great Suns, no abject commoners or wretched slaves. No one offered up kin to sacrifice. And if, as they developed, the southwest communities were less socially complex than those of the east, they nonetheless showed a high degree of technical and artistic proficiency.

The desert domain of the Hohokam—hot, low-lying, bone-dry most of the year—at first glance offered little encouragement to human habitation. Its single natural asset was a pair of rivers, later named the Gila and the Salt, which rose in the New Mexican mountains to the east and meandered through the sand flats on their way to the Gulf of California. The rivers were crucial. Each spring, when snow melted in the high country, they would overflow the banks and leave a deposit of alluvial silt. No land could have been more fertile. Thus, from around 300 BC, the Hohokam used this self-replenishing oasis to plant corn, beans, and squash, the staples of their diet.

The cultivation of corn was a Mexican specialty, and the Hohokam may have arrived as migrants from the long-established civilizations to the south. If so, they may also have imported the technology that allowed them to exploit the rivers' potential. For in their largely rainless land, only expert control of available river water and the runoff from arroyos could supply the moisture for serious agriculture.

At some indeterminate date, the Hohokam began to irrigate. Their first attempts were probably relatively modest—small dikes and shallow ditches leading to garden plots along the riverbanks. But from these crude beginnings, using no other tools than pointed digging sticks, the Hohokam proceeded to expand their system. Over the generations they built the dikes into large earthen dams, which diverted the current along main canals that reached thirty miles into the desert. Some channels were deepened to six feet or more and narrowed to retard evaporation. Water-resistant clay linings reduced seepage. An arrangement of movable baffles—thick mats of woven grass used to block off side channels—regulated water flow. The work went on century after century, and by the year 800, the Hohokam had constructed one of the most efficient, extensive irrigation networks in North America.

With water in relatively sure supply and dependable year-round sunshine, the Hohokam often were able to harvest two corn crops in a single year. The first, planted in March to take advantage of the spring runoff, came to ripeness in mid-July. Then another crop went in, just as thunderstorms in the mountains were bringing the river to a second flood. The harvested corn, dried on the ear, could be stored against future needs. With a hand-held rough stone, the Hohokam ground the kernels in an oblong, troughed stone, or metate. They mixed the resulting cornmeal with water and cooked it in a ceramic pot, adding to the gruel whatever greens and meat were available.

They may have planted the other main crops—squash and beans—in the same plots as the corn. By AD 500, they had added cotton, another gift from Mexico. In spite of their success as farmers, however, they depended on hunting and gathering for at least 50 percent of their food. Between harvests—and especially in dry years—they foraged in the desert for whatever it might provide. They found the fruits of the giant saguaro cactus and prickly pear nourishing, and ground the seedpods of the mesquite bush to make meal. They also gathered wild mustard, rhubarb, and pig-weed. In the strips of greenery along the riverbanks they could find enough small game to enrich the stewpot—muskrat, jack rabbit, various waterfowl. An occasional mule deer, pronghorn antelope, or mountain sheep provided a change of fare.

Life in a Hohokam settlement remained primitive and hard, nonetheless. Families lived in small huts with walls of slanting poles covered with clay and flimsy brush roofs. Each hut was set in a shallow depression where the loose desert soil had been scraped down to hardpan, thus creating a floor. Male householders maintained the canals and toiled in the fields, cultivating and harvesting. The women cooked, cared for the children, shaped and fired pottery vessels, and spent endless hours grinding corn into meal. Toolmakers used stone to flake stone, patiently shaping sharp edges onto the implements, and weavers made cloth from cotton and other fibers.

Yet the Hohokam had time for artistic endeavor. The earliest settlers decorated stone bowls with carved and painted animal forms, made pendants of shell and turquoise mosaic, and fashioned clay figurines for ritual use. Over time, both workmanship and design grew elaborate. An artisan at Snaketown, a settlement of at least 100 huts on the Gila River, sculpted a herd of nineteen deer, the animals each five inches high. Another potter, apparently with a keen sense of humor, produced an effigy pot in the shape of a fat-bellied man, whose nose doubled as a handle.

Like virtually every other group within reach of Mexican cultural influence, the Hohokam built earthen platforms for the enactment of ceremonial rites. Their platforms tended to be low, rectangular mounds of trash and rubble, which they paved over with adobe. Information on the nature of the rituals performed—whether rain dances, harvest festivals, or the investiture of leaders—would not survive. But the ceremonies apparently were benign compared with the stern and often bloody Mississippian rites. Neither the Hohokam nor any other southwestern people left any evidence that indicated they regularly indulged in ritual human slaughter.

But they probably did embrace the Mexican practice of playing ritual ball games—at least they built courts much like those in Mexico. As played in Mexico, the ball game was a rough-and-tumble contest that combined elements of soccer and a gang fight. Two teams squared off in a sunken court with sloping sides. Then, with knees, hips, and elbows—the use of hands and feet was forbidden—they would attempt to project a hard ball through a stone hoop on the wall. The Mexicans manufactured the balls of latex extracted from rubber trees in the Gulf Coast jungles. The Hohokam may have used the sap of a local plant, guayule, which grew in the desert, as well as imported rubber. In some cultures to the south, the losers of the game were sacrificed, but apparently not in the land of the Hohokam.

Late in the eighth century, when Mexican influence was at its strongest, the Hohokam entered a period of modest territorial expansion. The irrigation systems edged out along the Salt and Gila rivers and spilled into adjoining drainages. Hohokam farmers improved their techniques for cultivating maize, or corn, during this period. They also grew tobacco for smoking. And in this era, tribal artisans hit upon a new method for decorating shells. They covered parts of the surface in resinous pitch and subjected the unprotected areas to the acidic juice of a desert cactus—thus becoming the world's first etchers. (A similar technique would not be discovered in Europe until the fifteenth century.) But the tenor of life underwent little change during this period. The villagers dug their canals, harvested their corn, and conducted their ceremonies as they had for centuries. And they would continue doing so for the next 400 years.

While the Hohokam labored at their farming and handicrafts, their neighbors to the east, the Mogollon, probably devoted more of their time to hunting and foraging, a subsistence method dictated by the land. The steep valleys and rough escarpments of the Mogollon Mountains allowed limited space for planting crops. But the terrain did provide a variety of edible vegetation and wildlife. Lofty stands of ponderosa pine and occasional Douglas fir clad the north-facing slopes, their roots watered by the winter snows. Piñon pine, juniper, sage, berry bushes, and grasses stippled the lower slopes and southern exposures. The Mogollon gathered forty varieties of tasty, wild plants from the forests and upland meadows, either as food or as raw materials for tools, clothing, basket weaving, or other uses. To supplement the piñon nuts, black walnuts, and many other wild plant foods, they had game in abundance—rabbit, squirrel, beaver, muskrat, turkey, mule deer, and bighorn sheep. In addition to harvesting the natural bounty, each Mogollon family might tend a garden plot of corn and beans, planted from seeds obtained in trade with Hohokam lowlanders.

Few Mogollon settlements boasted more than a dozen small houses, which usually were scattered along isolated ridges offering unobstructed views of the countryside. The floors of the houses were set below ground level, as in the lowlands, but here the depressions were deeper and the sides of the excavated pit formed the lower portions of the house walls. The householder would dig the pit ten to sixteen feet across and some three to five feet deep, extend the walls above ground level with thatched sticks, then erect timber supports for a sloping roof of mud-daubed branches and thatch. Holes in the floor often provided storage, and a scooped-out area in the center served as the family hearth, from which the smoke drifted upward through a hole in the roof. In the harsh mountain climate, such a house provided natural year-round insulation, remaining cool in summer and snug against winter winds.

Some villages contained a pit house that was larger than the rest, where the men of the tribe could assemble. There, like the Mississippians, they smoked their stone pipes or reed cigarettes packed with tobacco, played a game with wooden dice, chipped tools and spear points from native stone, and fashioned snares and trip lines of plant fiber for capturing game. And there they laid plans for village festivals and tribal initiation rites. The men carved bone flutes and sculpted animal and human effigies in clay. Dancers and musicians adorned themselves in body paint—reds, blacks, and whites ground from colored stone. They robed themselves in cloaks of woven fur, cotton, or feathers, and aprons and girdles of yucca fiber. The women, meanwhile, concentrated their creative energies on more practical matters. It was they who wove baskets and sandals from the fibers of the yucca plant and who fashioned the dark red pottery and cooking utensils needed for daily living.

Simple and utilitarian, Mogollon culture enjoyed a long period of stable growth, and by the 700s, it had begun to trickle down from the mountains into the surrounding countryside. It spread into the Hohokam lands, where it was well received, and south into Mexico. And as the culture expanded it took on a veneer of unaccustomed sophistication. Around the second half of the tenth century, artisans in New Mexico's Mimbres Valley began fashioning a handsome black and white pottery that would rank among the highest expressions of indigenous American art. Agriculture took on greater importance in Mogollon life. At the same time villages grew more populous, with many householders moving above ground into multiroomed building complexes with walls of clay-plastered stone. In almost every respect, the Mogollon way of life was coming to resemble that of more advanced neighbors.

Although the Mogollon may have borrowed some ideas from the Hohokam, the new look in their domestic architecture resembled the work of the people directly to the north—the Anasazi of the Colorado Plateau. Relative latecomers to a sedentary, agricultural society, the Anasazi developed rapidly and would come to surpass all other southwest groups in the magnitude of their architectural achievements. Moreover, their legacy would continue, despite severe setbacks, into the era of European settlement, through their descendants, the Pueblo Indians.

The Anasazi dwelled in the high mesa country that later would be known as the

Bowls for the Dead

The most accomplished artisans among the peoples of the American southwest were peaceful villagers who lived for many centuries on irrigated strips of fertile land along the Mimbres River, in the arid southwestern corner of what would one day be New Mexico. Although they formed a branch of the Mogollon culture, the Mimbreño put their own distinctive stamp on their undertakings, especially the creation of vividly painted pottery such as that shown below and on the following pages. Decorated only in white combined with black or red, the pottery still manages to portray with stylized verve the creatures of the Mimbres world—the birds, animals, and insects that shared their desert environment; the mythic creatures of their religion; and their fellow humans. Most of their bowls were intended as offerings to be interred with the dead; some pieces were punctured—apparently "killed" ritually—as the holes in them would indicate.

The Mimbreño began to make the pottery in the middle of the seventh century. Their kilns poured forth these superb bowls and other vessels in great profusion, particularly from about AD 1000 to 1500. Then they ceased. Most likely the Mimbres River villages, reaching a population of about 2,500, outgrew the food supply. Forced to migrate, the people may have sought haven and sustenance in other Mogollon communities, their special skills and styles melting away in the process. In any case, the distinctive culture of the Mimbreño was seen no more.

RABBIT WITH CEREMONIAL WAND

FOUR FISH

Four Corners—the area around the juncture of Colorado, Utah, Arizona, and New Mexico. Less arid than the Hohokam desert, not quite as rugged as the Mogollon Mountains, it was nevertheless harsh—a place of vast, undulating tablelands cut by narrow gorges and bleak, sandstone ridges, with thin soils that supported woodlands of piñon and juniper and valleys of greasewood and bunch grass. The part of the area that lay above 7,500 feet might be too cold to grow corn some summers, and the land below 5,500 feet was sometimes too dry and searingly hot for the grain. But in the intermediate elevations and along canyon bottoms where streams fed oases of grass, cottonwood, and willow there was promise for agriculture.

The Anasazi's ancestors had entered this landscape as hunters, pursuing pronghorn antelope, mule deer, mountain sheep, and an occasional buffalo. At first they sheltered in caves in the rocky cliffs and canyon walls. Lacking pottery, they made do with baskets woven tightly enough to hold water. Then, sometime around the fifth or sixth century AD, Anasazi life took a sharp turn in direction. The people began to make pots. They became more dependent on corn, learning to produce greater yields and, for the first time, storing substantial amounts of it over the winter for year-round use. And they moved into their first true houses.

LIZARD

BIRD

Posterity was to have no clear understanding of the inspiration for these improvements. Possibly, Anasazi hunting parties, tracking south across the plateau, encountered their Mogollon neighbors, from whom they may have learned some new agricultural techniques. Their pottery, too, was a puzzlement. Much of it was crudely utilitarian, in unadorned basketlike shapes most likely inspired by Mogollon examples. But some vessels decorated with human figures showed a flamboyance that was amazingly akin to the work of eastern potters. And the early Anasazi houses, dome-shaped structures of mud-plastered logs laid horizontally around saucerlike excavations, were unique in the southwest.

Like so much about the early Americans, the origins of these Anasazi features would be obscure to later generations. Perhaps the expanding Mississippi culture rolled across the prairies to leave its mark in the canyon lands. Or perhaps the resemblances were coincidental, and the Anasazi developed these basic cultural elements on their own. Whatever they did borrow, they soon improved upon. The early log houses gave way to pit houses like those of the Mogollon, which the Anasazi fitted out with paved floors, interior stone wainscoting, and sometimes, partitions sectioning the interior. Eventually, the Anasazi's improved farming methods pro-

TURE WITH BIRD HEAD AND FISH TAIL

GEOMETRIC DESIGN

MYTHIC DANCER WITH HELMET HEAD

duced surplus corn, which was stored in aboveground granaries—structures of clay-plastered branches and twigs at first, then bins of closely fitted stone.

As masonry techniques improved, the Anasazi engineered a great advance in domestic architecture. Like other peoples around the world before and since, they found they needed spaces differentiated for specialized activities and uses inside their dwellings—areas for storage, for sleeping, for cooking and eating. A pit house could be subdivided only so far before the spaces became too small. Around AD 750, the Anasazi began to move above ground, taking up residence in masonry buildings with many rooms arranged in a long line or arc. The line of rooms faced the old pit houses, which were retained possibly for ceremonial use and because they provided warmer shelter in very cold weather. By AD 800, the Anasazi were constructing the first multistory pueblos—massive, stone apartment compounds that contained scores of rooms to accommodate numerous people and their belongings.

The next two centuries saw a dramatic rise in living standards and population. The climate may have moderated, bringing moister, more temperate summers in which crop yields swelled. Farmers installed a system of check dams and storage ponds at the canyon heads in order to conserve water from the spring thaw and midsummer

GEOMETRIC DESIGN

BIRD AND FISH

thunderstorms. As a consequence, more land was now brought under cultivation.

A few new tools and techniques accompanied the rising prosperity. Stone shapers cut axheads with grooves for the thongs that bound them onto wooden handles. The wild turkey was tamed and raised in the pueblos for meat and also for feathers, which gave a flourish to ceremonial regalia. Anasazi artisans constructed wooden looms for weaving garments of cotton, a plant acquired from the Hohokam. Other crafts reached new levels. Shell bracelets, beads of turquoise and other gemstones, bone scrapers with turquoise inlay, carved ornaments of imported abalone shell added glitter to Anasazi life. And potters produced the ornamental black-on-white ware that would inspire the Mogollon ceramic workers of the Mimbres Valley and elsewhere.

But the pueblos remained the supreme Anasazi achievement. At least a dozen Great Houses took shape below the bluffs of Chaco Canyon in northwest New Mexico, each one a virtual stone town (which is why the Spanish would later call them pueblos, the Spanish word for towns). They were built with four-foot-thick masonry walls and adjoining apartments to accommodate scores, even hundreds, of families. The largest, later named Pueblo Bonito, rose in five, terraced stories, contained more than 800 rooms, and could have housed a population of 1,000 or more.

Besides living quarters, each pueblo included one or more kivas—circular underground chambers faced with stone that strongly recalled the early Anasazi pit houses and the Mogollon lodge houses. Their function was in fact the same, for they were all-male sanctuaries where elders met to plan festivals, perform ritual dances, settle pueblo affairs, and impart tribal lore to the younger generation. Some kivas were enormous. Of the thirty or so at Pueblo Bonito, two measured sixty feet across. They contained niches for ceremonial objects, a central fire pit, and holes in the floor for communicating with the spirits of tribal ancestors.

Each pueblo represented an astonishing amount of well-organized labor. Using only stone and wood tools, and without benefit of wheels or draft animals, the builders quarried ton upon ton of sandstone from the canyon walls, cut it into small blocks, hauled the blocks to the construction site, and fitted them together with mud mortar. Roof beams of pine or fir had to be carried from logging areas in the mountain forests many miles away. Then, to connect the pueblos and to give access to the surrounding tableland, the architects laid out a system of public roads with stone staircases for ascending cliff faces. In time, the roads reached out to more than eighty satellite villages within a 100-mile radius.

The Chaco builders moved into their most energetic phase toward the end of the tenth century, and they continued to thrive for nearly 300 more years. Meanwhile, other Anasazi groups to the west and north began shaping their own form of pueblo existence. At Canyon de Chelly in Arizona and at Mesa Verde in southwestern Colorado, the first stone apartment compounds took shape on the canyon rims. But future generations would build in caverns and crevices within the cliffs themselves, high above the bottomlands and shielded from above by the overhanging rimrock. Perhaps the northern Anasazi came under savage assault by nomadic warrior tribes from the Great Plains and selected their inaccessible perches for protection. Whatever the reason, as a feat of architectural engineering the northern cliff dwellings rivaled the achievement of the Chaco masters, and they would stand to astonish visitors for nearly a thousand years after the last stones were laid.

As the peoples of the southwest were beginning to taste the amenities of civilized life,

145

THE CLIFF DWELLERS OF MESA VERDE

Possibly for protection from marauding tribes of the plains, the Anasazi people of the desert southwest built their villages in the most inaccessible places that the terrain offered them—within the walls of the deep canyons that abounded in their native region. Among these fortresslike cliff dwellings, none was more remote than the one shown here, the great pueblo built sometime around AD 1200 in a fertile corner of southern Colorado that would later be known by Spanish explorers as Mesa Verde, or "Green Table."

The greenness was literally on top of the village—a fertile strip of plateau high above a precipitous canyon. There, Mesa Verde's people cultivated plots of corn, beans, and squash between copses of piñon and juniper trees. The village itself—a rambling, stone structure encompassing more than 200 rooms that housed the entire community—lay partway down the sheer canyon wall. The complex was tucked into a vast crevice, 325 feet long and 90 feet deep, that lay 500 feet above the canyon floor. The only way in or out of the village was via steep paths—some no more than a precarious series of toeholds—cut in the 100-foot-tall rock face above.

the ancient city-states of Middle America were slipping into a period of turbulent decline. At the beginning of the ninth century, the great metropolis of Teotihuacán, once source and arbiter of Mexico's strongest cultural energies, lay abandoned; around AD 750, its shrines and pyramids had been ransacked and burned, its people massacred or dispersed by unknown attackers. Teotihuacán's collapse had left a vacuum in central Mexico, where a handful of lesser states now jostled for supremacy. In the jungles to the southeast, near the Gulf Coast and in the Guatemalan lowlands, the ornate ceremonial centers of the Maya were reaching their flamboyant apogee. But in little more than a century they, too, would fall into ruin. Everywhere, the harmonious balance of Middle America's classic period, the era of its loftiest cultural achievements, was giving way to bloodshed, disruption, and decay.

The decline was by no means uniform, however. At the opening of the ninth century, dozens of Mayan communities were springing up in the hills and plains of the Yucatan Peninsula. At such places as Uxmal, Labná, and Sayil in the Puuc Hills, the Maya began constructing the ceremonial compounds that were essential to their rituals. The result was a second Mayan cultural flowering of major proportions. Among its legacies were new styles in architecture particularly suited to the Yucatan's more open terrain. No longer did the builders feel compelled to raise their temple pyramids 200 feet or more to reach above a dense forest canopy. And what they sacrificed in height, they made up in solid, monumental breadth and in ornamentation. Fronting ceremonial plazas were majestic palaces decorated with geometric designs of stone blocks, precut to standard sizes. At Uxmal, the 320-foot-long Palace of the Governor was crowned by a magnificent geometric-patterned limestone frieze—radically different from the old Mayan surface decorations of painted stucco figures that twined together like so much jungle foliage.

The Puuc Maya demonstrated an increased attention to elaborate public display, but the basic rituals remained the same as in previous centuries. Rulers continued to mutilate their bodies in the belief that the flow of royal blood would nourish the gods. Captive enemies were offered up in sacrifice, their hearts carved from their chests. And Mayan sages went on plotting the trajectories of the planets, refining their calendars, and recording the dynastic sagas of royal families in bark-paper booklets.

While some Yucatan communities were devoted to scholarship and religion, others seem to have filled more of a commercial function. As many as 100,000 people may have resided at Dzibilchaltún, a trading center near the peninsula's northern coast, where the inhabitants crowded into a warren of twisting alleyways and tightly packed, stone houses. An energetic seagoing trade was dominated by Mayan entrepreneurs from the Putún region to the west. The merchants would set out from Xicallanco, the main Putún port, in canoes, circle east to Dzibilchaltún, then paddle south along the coast as far as Naco in Honduras, nearly 1,000 miles from home.

Yet throughout Middle America, peaceful trade was frequently interrupted by war. Among the groups competing for power and territory were the Mixtec, who lived in small mountain villages north and west of the Valley of Oaxaca in southern Mexico. Known as the Cloud People—their ancestors, according to legend, had descended from the skies to the crags of their homeland—the Mixtec were proud, brave, and endowed with great artistic talent. Mixtec goldsmiths and potters produced some of America's most exquisite and imaginative works. But the Mixtec were also adept at battle. Around AD 950, the Mixtec marched south into Oaxaca to challenge the Zapotec of Monte Albán, winning control of that thousand-year-old city. Other

A man's head emerges from the jaws of a coyote in this haunting piece of Toltec sculpture, which probably represents Coyotlinaual, principal deity of the hereditary guild of featherworkers in the Toltec capital of Tollan in central Mexico. The figure was crafted of pottery overlaid with a mosaic of mother-of-pearl incised to resemble feathers. The face appears to have a beard, an artistic convention usually reserved for depictions of gods or revered leaders. The featherworkers' guild was but one of many such craft associations—each with its own patron deity—in the organized culture of the Toltec.

Colossal warriors dressed in full battle gear *(above)* reflect the extreme militarism of the Toltec. The carved stone columns once supported a temple roof in Tollan. Reclining figures such as the one at left, from Chichén Itzá on the Yucatan Peninsula, bore receptacles for sacrificial offerings; statuary of this sort appeared wherever the Toltec settled.

Mixtec warriors went north toward the urban centers bordering the Valley of Mexico.

Perhaps the most powerful Mixtec leader was a chieftain known as Eight-Deer Ocelot-Claw. (Every day of the Mixtec calendar had a number and name, and like most Mixtec children, Eight-Deer Ocelot-Claw was named first for his birth date, Eight-Deer day. He was awarded his other name, Ocelot-Claw, after becoming leader of his people.) Ruler of his clan by age nineteen, he proved proficient at both combat and intrigue. And by means of a string of successful campaigns and judicious marriages, he soon extended his power across the Mixtec highlands and down to the Pacific coast. He tolerated no opposition. When the succession to the throne of a far-distant city was in doubt, Eight-Deer captured all the candidates, including his own half brother Twelve-Earthquake, and sacrificed them to the gods. Such exploits were devoutly recorded on deerskin in Mixtec picture writing. Then in 1063, when he had reached the ripe age of fifty-two, Eight-Deer himself was captured in battle and expired on the sacrificial altar of an enemy chieftain.

The tribal groups in the central Mexico region formerly controlled by the great city of Teotihuacán, meanwhile, were showing an inclination to assimilate traits from various peoples and to synthesize them into a new, composite culture. The people inhabiting the hilltop bastion of Xochicalco, located in rolling farmland south of the Valley of Mexico, became particularly cosmopolitan in outlook, blending cultural elements from all over Mexico.

Xochicalco's lofty setting and many of the glyphs carved on its stones, identical to glyphs used in Zapotec picture writing, were evocative of Monte Albán, the Zapotecs' old, mountaintop capital. But Xochicalco boasted a temple pyramid, stone-paved causeways, a sweat bath, and a court for the ritual American ball game that had a clearly Mayan stylistic flourish, including carvings of human figures seated in traditional Mayan positions. The city apparently had trading ties with the Maya, as it did with the people of the Valley of Mexico, Guerrero, Oaxaca, and other areas. Xochicalco seemed to take in whatever styles and practices pleased it.

A similar hub of cosmopolitan life was Cacaxtla, a mountaintop settlement halfway between the Valley of Mexico and the Gulf Coast. This city absorbed elements of style from Xochicalco, from Teotihuacán, from the lowland Maya, and from the Gulf Coast settlements in the area that later would be called Veracruz. The city of Cholula—a commercial and religious center notable for its vast pyramid, one of the largest ever built in ancient America—was close by. But the Cholulans were fierce and successful warriors who maintained their independence from Cacaxtla.

The tribes of the Veracruz region along the Gulf coast were every bit as robust and ambitious as their neighbors. The regional capital, which the Spanish much later would name El Tajín, crowned two parallel ridges fifteen miles inland and overlooked miles of undulating farmland planted in corn, cotton, beans, vanilla, and cocoa. Grown rich on farming, trade, and—probably—warfare, El Tajín held sway over people throughout the Gulf area and the neighboring highlands. At the pinnacle of its power, from around 600 to 900, the city encompassed more than 2,500 acres. And the leading activity of its citizens, aside from harvesting their crops and collecting tribute, was a particularly vigorous cult of sacrifice and death. A group of temple pyramids studded the ceremonial center on El Tajín's main ridge, along with palaces, administrative buildings, ball courts, and a marketplace. Multitiered structures with overhanging cornices and windowlike niches, the temples were adorned with a menagerie of stone carvings: toads, jaguars, serpents, and human skulls. Among the most frequent motifs, appearing everywhere, was the skeletal visage of the Death God.

Candidates for sacrifice were selected, in part, by the outcome of the ritual ball game, played on eleven ball courts of varying sizes. In the past, some cities had played the game for lower stakes—to settle political disputes, for example. But in this era, at least in El Tajín, it was a prelude to death. After the game, at least one of the players would be escorted to the executioner's block—possibly the vanquished captain, perhaps the leader of the winning team, maybe a preselected victim whose team followed a prearranged plan to win or lose in what was more of a drama than a sporting contest. He might be offered an intoxicating draft of pulque, fermented from the juice of the maguey plant. Then he was ritually beheaded, or the priests might pluck his heart from his body instead. Such a death was highly honorable. Only noblemen were eligible to compete in the games, and the victim earned semidivine status, for he was being entrusted with a message to the gods. He was buried with the highest distinction, probably with a jade bead set in his mouth and his body placed upon a U-shaped yoke of carved stone. This sacred totem resembled the wood and leather waist piece he had worn in the ball court, and it represented the jaws of the earth demon who guarded the gates of the underworld.

The cities of central Mexico gradually fell into decline after about AD 900, aggressive to the end, but now victims of a shift of power. A new, militarily strong culture was emerging to the north, in the arid highlands beyond the Valley of Mexico, and it would shortly thrust the older civilizations into eclipse. Primitive people called Chichimecs—Sons of the Dog—swept out of the desert to ravage the valley settlements. Some of the invaders were turned back, or departed of their own accord, laden with loot and captives. But at least one group, the Toltec, remained.

According to legend, the Toltec roamed the valley, led by a tribal patriarch named Mixcoatl, or Cloud-Serpent. They settled briefly at Culhuacán, a few miles south of where Mexico City one day would rise, and picked up a smattering of the old regional culture. Then, the story goes, Mixcoatl died, leaving the tribal leadership to his son Topiltzin. Whether an actual Mixcoatl ever existed, Topiltzin was definitely a real person. He led his people north, to the plateau just beyond the valley rim. The area was agreeable and there he founded a city—Tollan, the Place of the Reeds—on a rise overlooking a small river. (The Spanish would later corrupt the name of the city to Tula.) At this spot the Toltec remained and began to make their presence felt.

Much of Toltec history would be handed on in legends recited by their imperial successors, the Aztec, who would control the Valley of Mexico in the fourteenth century. And like most oral tradition, the tales would mingle fact with mythic fabrication. In Aztec belief, the Toltec were masters in every endeavor—superb artisans, expert farmers, invincible warriors, all-wise statesmen. "Nothing was too difficult for them," according to Aztec oral tradition, "no place with which they dealt too distant." The Tollan of legend was pictured as a paradise where the ears of corn grew as big as grinding stones, where kings lived in palaces of jade and gold, and where potters were so skillful they "taught the clay to lie."

Topiltzin settled in Tollan around AD 950, leading not only his Toltec warriors but also a large subject population of Nonoalca, or Deaf and Dumb People—so-called presumably because they could not speak or understand the language of the Toltec. The Nonoalca seem to have come from all over the Valley of Mexico and beyond, and they included a large work force of architects, sculptors, painters, and laborers. It was they who, under Topiltzin's direction, imbued Tollan with a rough, eclectic majesty drawn from other Mexican cultures. The city's ball court, for example, was an exact replica of the one at Xochicalco. And there were representations of Quetzalcoatl, whom the Toltec adopted as the city's patron deity, that seem to have been copied directly from the ruins of Teotihuacán.

But stern new figures crowded in among the ancient images, reflecting the Toltec's militant nature. The giant columns that supported the roof of the most impressive temple were shaped like colossal warriors, each carrying an atlatl in one hand and what might be a sheaf of arrows in the other. These seemed to represent a class of professional warriors who gave the Toltec realm its power. Motifs of regiments or warrior societies—jaguars, coyotes, and eagles—adorned the temple's base.

And reminders of ritual human sacrifice abounded among the images at Tollan. A row of eagles adorned one wall, each gnawing a human heart. The temples contained sacred vessels that held the hearts of sacrificial victims. Beside one ball court stood an altar marked with skulls and crossbones; there the Toltec placed the heads of sacrificial victims. And a large reclining stone figure with a tray on its belly was used to display a human heart while it was still throbbing. Wherever these so-called chacmools appeared in Mexico, they were a sign of Toltec influence.

The bloodier artifacts at Tollan may have been the work of Topiltzin's successors. Sometime during the founder's middle years, revolution rocked the capital as a rival faction attempted to grasp control. Religion played a crucial role in the outcome. Topiltzin—who had also taken the name of Quetzalcoatl, the ancient feathered serpent god—was a god-priest of the dominant state cult as well as the ruler. He was revered for his wisdom, piety, and celibacy; he had never lain with a woman. The rebellious faction worshiped Tezcatlipoca, Smoking Mirror, deity of sorcery and war, the giver and taker of life. According to legend, Smoking Mirror, unable to win by fair means, resorted to foul. Appearing at court in the guise of a harmless old man, he offered Topiltzin-Quetzalcoatl a magic elixir. The king tasted it, liked it, and downed the entire draft. Crazed by the potion, the heretofore virginal god-king was persuaded to ravish his sister. The next morning, when he realized his awful sacrilege, Topiltzin departed Tollan with his retainers for self-imposed exile.

Topiltzin-Quetzalcoatl repaired to Cholula, where he remained for twenty years, and then set out on a journey to the east. In one legend, he put to sea on a raft made of serpents. In another, he hurled himself on a funeral pyre and rose to heaven to become the Morning Star, the god Quetzalcoatl's celestial manifestation. In both cases, he promised to return at a date that, by European reckoning, would be the year 1519—at which point he would usher in a glorious age. The legend would have profound consequences. For by one of the most remarkable and fateful coincidences of all time, 1519 would see the arrival of the Spanish conquistadores on the shore of Mexico. Because of the legend, they would be hailed as returning gods by the Americans—who had no notion they were welcoming their own doom.

Around the time of Topiltzin's departure, Tollan embarked on its most vigorous period of conquest. Toltec armies, probably recruited from a number of different tribes and cities, spread out to dominate most of Mexico. Their most spectacular advance was to the east—led, it so happened, by another chieftain who also was named Quetzalcoatl. His forces invaded Yucatan around AD 1000 and soon overran the peninsula, subduing the Puuc Mayan settlements. He established his headquarters at the Mayan city of Chichén Itzá, where he imposed the fierce warrior cult of skulls, jaguar warrior societies, chacmools, and human sacrifice. Tollan, meanwhile,

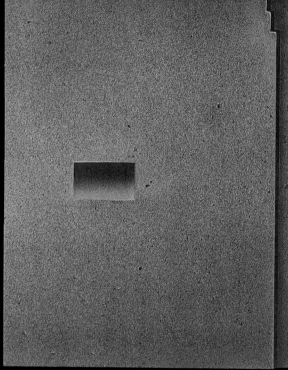

Intricate carvings of the Staff-Bearing God and his attendants adorn the lintel of the Gateway of the Sun *(above)* in Tiahuanaco, the ancient city in the Andes. The Staff-Bearing God was the supreme deity of the Tiahuanacans, and his characteristic motifs became familiar throughout the Andean world: the god's tears, his headdress, the two staffs, as well as the stylized animal-like attendants. Seven hundred miles away in Peru similar attributes were ascribed to a god pictured on the two sides of a ceremonial urn *(left and right)* crafted by a people called the Huari.

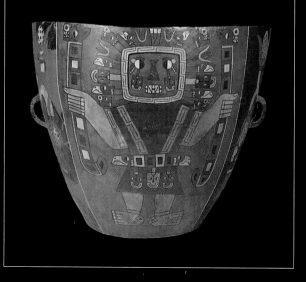

continued to thrive for another 150 years, growing into a metropolis of 30,000 souls. Then, in the twelfth century, the great city fell, perhaps overpowered by yet another wave of primitive nomads from the north, and the Toltec empire crumbled into ruin.

Some 5,000 miles to the south, in the cold, thin air of the Bolivian Andes, another American civilization was coming into magnificent, final flower. A giant cluster of palaces and temples rose over the treeless, high plateau twelve miles south of Lake Titicaca and 12,500 feet above sea level, the massive blocks of cut and polished stone gleaming in the mountain sun. This was the great ceremonial and political capital of Tiahuanaco, one of the the most powerful cultural forces in all South America.

To travelers from the lowlands, Tiahuanaco must have appeared as the work of titans. A visitor approached the city's ceremonial center through a monumental gateway carved from a single block of stone, its surface swarming with occult patterns and religious figures. Beyond lay a progression of huge terraces, broad, sunken courtyards, and temples adorned with totemistic stone heads. Enormous stone sentinels, some as tall as twenty-five feet, peered down, scrutinizing all who passed by.

The largest temple platform was 50 feet high and measured 656 feet square at its base. Some of the stones weighed more than 100 tons and had been dragged by work brigades from quarries more than three miles away. Each block was shaped to a smooth, precise finish, and many had been set into place without mortar. So exact was the fit of some blocks that a blade of grass would not slide between them. Nevertheless, certain key stones were clamped together with bronze or copper fittings—a sensible precaution in a land of frequent earthquakes.

Over all loomed the stern and forbidding image of Tiahuanaco's patron deity, the Staff-Bearing God. The god's stony-faced, staring-eyed countenance presided everywhere; he was the largest figure depicted on the Gateway of the Sun and was shown in the highest, dominant position there. His brow was crowned with a halo of solarlike rays, and tracks of tears ran down his cheeks. He was pictured carrying a staff, which sometimes was formed of snakes and sometimes of corn stalks or other crops. The snakes probably represented lightning bolts and the corn, fertility. Tiahuanaco's powerful Staff-Bearing God, as his widely scattered images indicated, had cast his spell far up the spine of the Andes, down to the villages of the Pacific coast, and indeed, across virtually all of the region's most ancient peoples.

Tiahuanaco's rise to greatness had begun around AD 500, propelled in part by religious energy and in part by growing economic might. For all its stark location, the city enjoyed some particular natural advantages. The plateau was well suited for high-altitude farming based on such cold-resistant plants as the potato, the oca (a tuber resembling the sweet potato), and also a ricelike, protein-rich grain called quinoa. Nearby Lake Titicaca yielded fish and waterfowl in abundance. Most of all, the surrounding grasslands were the natural habitat of South America's two most valued animals, the wooly-haired alpaca and its cousin the llama. From the alpaca's wool and from cotton, the Tiahuanacans wove handsome tapestry tunics and pile hats. The llama provided a coarser wool, as well as hides, meat, and uniquely, transport. Until the coming of the Spanish horse, it was the Americas' only beast of burden, able to carry up to ninety pounds of cargo over treacherous mountain trails.

The Tiahuanacans thus became South America's most important livestock breeders, and this in turn allowed them to run a trade monopoly in the central Andes. Their llama caravans threaded their way down through the foothills to the Pacific coast and over the high passes to the rain forests of the eastern slopes. The beasts carried corn, seashells, tropical feathers, medicinal plants, and coca, a narcotic leaf chewed to counteract the fatigue common in the thin, high-altitude atmosphere.

To augment their power—and increase their riches—the Tiahuanacan rulers sent groups to establish colonies throughout the region. The purpose of these centers was to acquire and to ship back to the capital any desired raw materials or trade goods. Nor did the city rulers neglect Tiahuanaco's agriculture. A program of land reclamation transformed the shores of Lake Titicaca, as teams of laborers drained marshes and built areas of fertile landfill. Large outlying communities, handsomely appointed with cut-stone temples and statuary like that in the capital, were founded to marshal work forces and to collect tribute. The wealth poured in. By AD 800, Tiahuanaco was a thriving metropolis of perhaps 40,000 people.

The influence of Tiahuanaco's religious cult extended far beyond the city's political power. Some 600 miles to the north, in Peru's 9,000-foot-high Ayachuco Valley, the independent empire of the Huari was ruled from an equally impressive capital. Even larger than Tiahuanaco, Huari covered 1,200 acres and housed as many as 70,000 people, making it one of the most densely populated urban centers in the western hemisphere. Like Tiahuanaco, Huari was a center of commerce and worship. There was a ceremonial quarter with temples, tombs, and palaces for the elite. Another section contained housing complexes for commoners. In a separate precinct, artisans turned out multicolored woolen tapestries, copper and gold jewelry, stone figurines inlaid with precious metals and colored shells, and ceramic vessels painted a wide range of colors, including black, white, red, gray, yellow, and purple.

Huari building techniques were distinct from those of Tiahuanaco. The Huari fashioned dwellings and temples from fieldstone set in mud mortar and smoothed over with coats of clay and plaster. The walls were massive, from three to six feet thick, some standing thirty or forty feet high and supporting two or three stories. The Huari seem to have lacked the extraordinary stonecutting skill of the Tiahuanaco masters, however, and only in a few royal tombs did they attempt to duplicate it.

All in all, the Huari were their own people. Except in one respect. Beginning around 600, the image of Tiahuanaco's Staff-Bearing God began appearing with increasing frequency on Huari artifacts. It glared out from tapestry garments and from urns, jars, and tumblers at Huari sites all over Peru. Often the god was shown with a pair of staffs in the form of writhing snakes. Another image common to both the Tiahuanacan and Huari areas was a sacrificer, often shown with a knife and severed human heads. When this figure or the Staff-Bearing God showed up in a Huari community, it was a sign that Tiahuanaco's religious ideas had taken root.

About the same time that the Huari adopted the Staff-Bearing God, they also embarked on a series of military conquests. They swallowed up the region's local tribal states one after another—the Nazca, the Moche, and several more—until they controlled Peru from the Andean peaks to the coastal deserts. In so doing, they replaced the ancient cultural diversity with a unified Huari-Tiahuanaco style and created what was probably the first centralized military empire in South America.

Huari supremacy lasted more than 200 years. Then in the ninth century, for reasons unknown, it abruptly collapsed. Tiahuanaco continued to exercise its influence for about three more centuries. By around the year 1200, it too would fade into obscurity. Yet together, the two imperial states had laid the foundation for a new Andes empire, that of the Incas, which would rise to glory a few centuries later.

The most extraordinary artisans among the New World's peoples were the goldsmiths of ancient South and Central America. Working initially with little more than crude stone hammers to shape the ore and bone awls to emboss it, they produced gleaming religious totems and jewel-like ornaments that were as beautiful and sophisticated as the finest goldwork achieved by the most advanced civilizations across the oceans in Europe and Asia.

The first to work the lustrous metal, not surprisingly, were craftsmen belonging to the several cultures that flourished in Peru, where the geological forces that formed the Andes range had packed the mountains with more gold than could be found in any other region on earth. The Peruvian smiths began by pounding their plentiful nuggets into thin sheets, which they cut and embossed into bold and haunting designs. By the time the Vikings were ravaging Europe, however, the Peruvians had found ways to bend and solder the sheets into graceful rounded forms portraying animals and humans, deities and demons.

Meanwhile, goldworking had moved up the Andean chain from Peru into what would become Ecuador and Colombia and from there across the Isthmus of Panama to Costa Rica and southern Mexico. Some of these later artisans made astonishing tech-

nological discoveries. They learned to concoct subtle alloys, mixing gold with copper for strength or with precious platinum for added brilliance. More amazingly, they duplicated in their forest clearings the most ingenious artistic breakthrough of Middle Eastern antiquity, the lost-wax process. Using soft beeswax, a native American smith would make an intricately detailed model of an ornament, encase the model in a clay mold, and heat the mold until the wax melted away. Then the smith poured molten gold into the mold's now empty cavity, waited for it to cool, and broke open the clay form to extract a magically exact copy of the wax original—a finished article such as the flying-fish pendant shown above.

Little of the magnificent goldwork found by the Spanish survived the conquests of Central and South America of the 1500s. Crazed with gold fever, the Spaniards melted into bullion virtually every gold object they found. From the hoard of a single Peruvian king they took 13,420 pounds of the metal. But a few masterworks made it to Spain intact, causing one awestruck European notable to exclaim, "I never saw anything whose beauty might so allure the eye of man." More items that the Spaniards missed have been unearthed since—including those shown on the following pages—to allure the eyes of later generations.

A golden beaker, turned upside down, shows the fierce visage of a deity of Peru's Sicán people. The beaker was made of a thick sheet of gold rough-shaped by hammering over a wooden block. The slanted eyes, fanglike teeth, and other features were added by further hammering over a carved wooden form. The imperfect nose clearly caused trouble and had to be patched.

This elegant Sicán ceremonial beaker has a false bottom, marked by the cross-shaped holes, containing pellets that rattle when the vessel is shaken. Above the turquoise inlays, a band of animal forms with large round eyes and birdlike mouths decorate the cup. This beaker, like the one at left, was shaped over a mold; the false bottom, made separately, was crimped into place.

A triumph of the jeweler's art, the handle of the ceremonial knife at left combines semiprecious stones with scores of gold beads and many pieces of sheet gold, shaped separately and then joined by crimping or soldering. Above the face of the Sicán dignitary—probably a king or deity—the elaborate, fanned-out headdress bears a rough turquoise, which is echoed by the turquoise disks below and the smaller, gold-rimmed earplugs. As a final touch, the goldsmith added four tiny birds marching down the sides of the handle.

In a magnificent offering
to the gods, the golden
figure of a king, bedecked
with elaborate gold jewelry and accompanied by
half a dozen attendants,
sits on an openwork raft
woven of hammered gold
strips and threads. Made
by the Muisca people who
lived in what is now Co-
lombia, such offerings
were thrown into a small
Andean lake near present-
day Bogota whenever a
new ruler was installed
on the throne. This
eight-inch-long master-
piece was cast using the
lost-wax method.

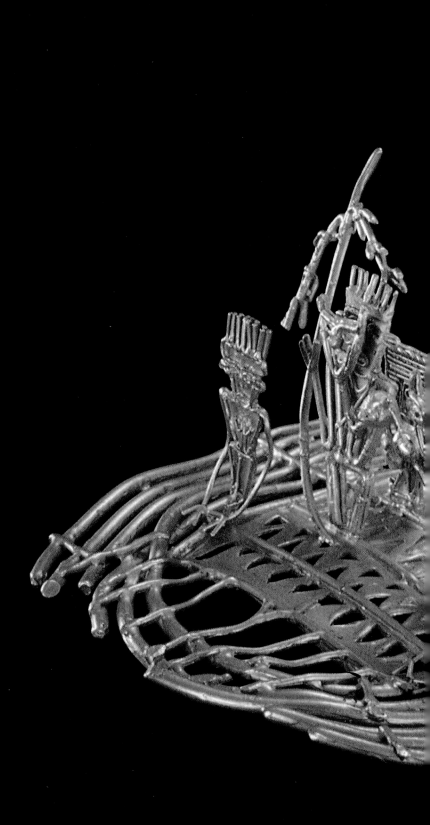

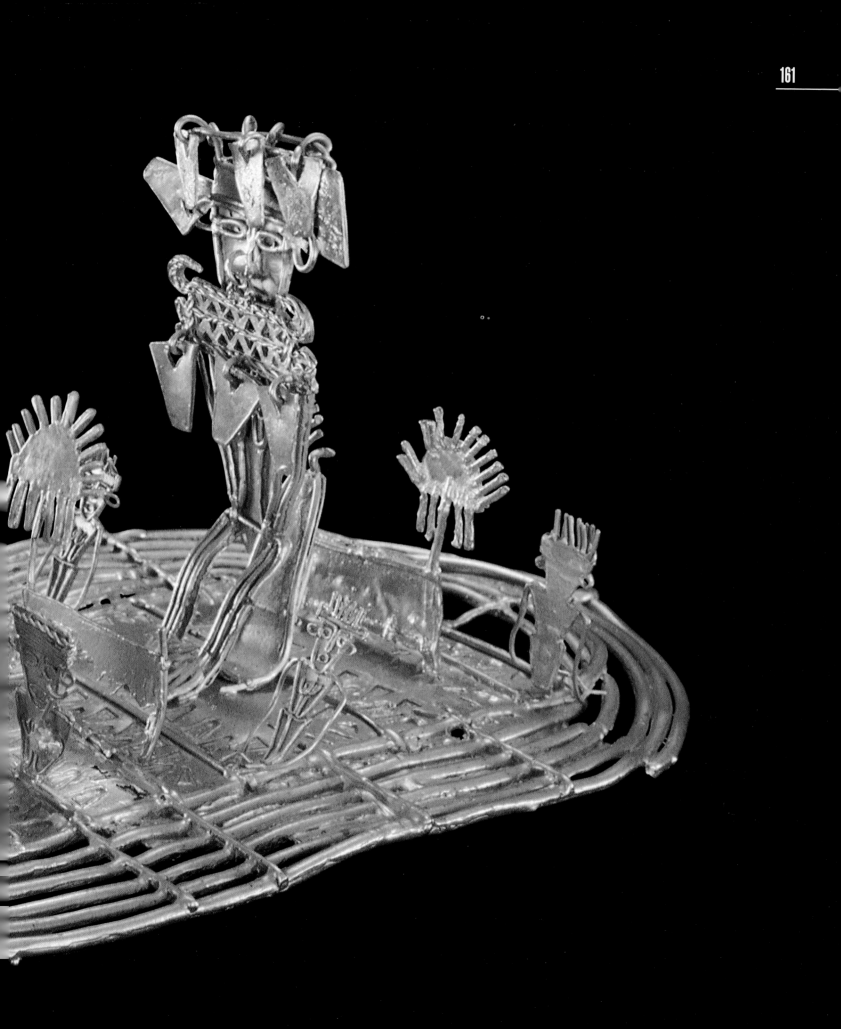

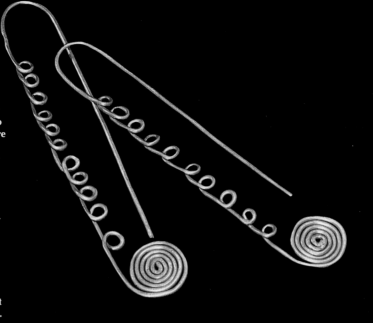

The five-inch-long ornaments for pierced ears *(right)* were fashioned by Calima artisans, who first hammered sheet gold into wire, then twisted the wire into loops with a decorative spiral at the end. The beautifully balanced and symmetrical nose piece shown below was crafted in the high Andes region of Colombia along the Ecuadorian border, where the goldsmiths favored abstract designs. Such ornaments, popular among native South Americans, were worn clipped to the septum of the nose so that they hung over the mouth.

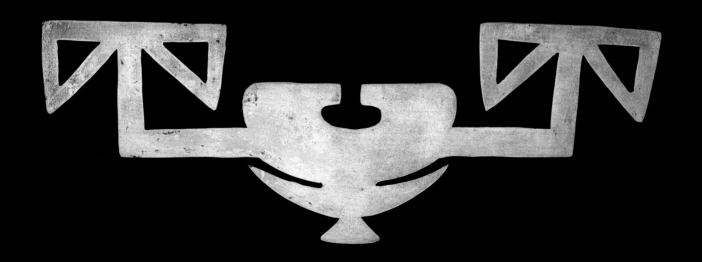

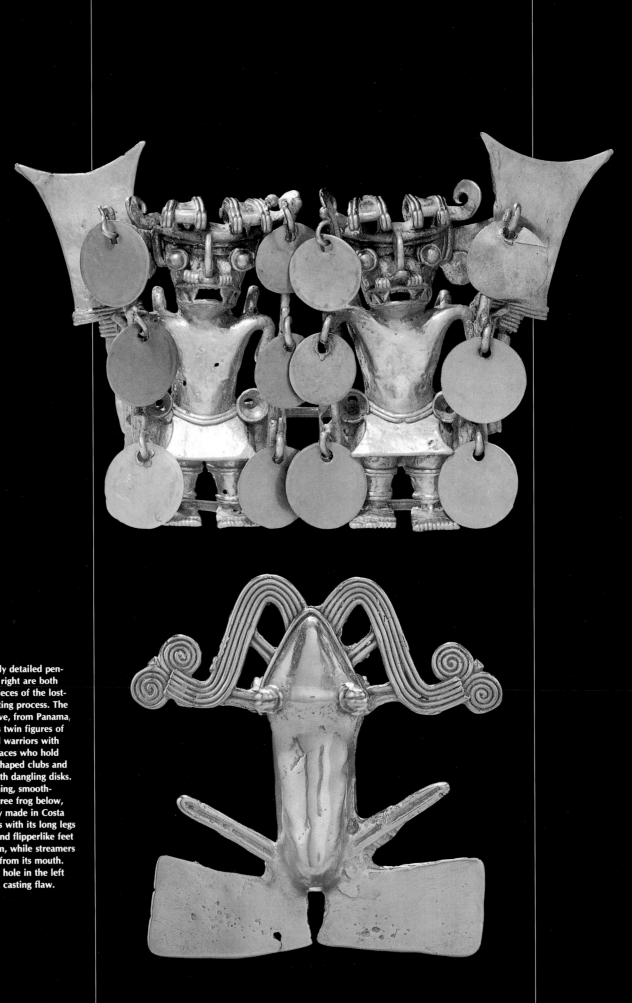

The richly detailed pendants at right are both masterpieces of the lost-wax casting process. The one above, from Panama, balances twin figures of mythical warriors with batlike faces who hold paddle-shaped clubs and poles with dangling disks. The shining, smooth-bodied tree frog below, probably made in Costa Rica, sits with its long legs folded and flipperlike feet tucked in, while streamers emerge from its mouth. The tiny hole in the left foot is a casting flaw.

The chest ornament at left, crafted of flat, pounded gold by artisans who probably lived in southwestern Colombia, appears plain and abstract—except for the small human face with oval eyes, a broad nose, narrow lips, and a goatee that appears in the middle of the crossbar. The features are barely suggested—the head is not defined at all—but they serve to convert the shape into the body and outstretched arms of a man, giving the ornament a subtle, haunting power.

This huge funerary mask from Peru probably accompanied the body of a deceased king or powerful nobleman to its final resting place. The mask, 24¾ inches wide, has spangles on its upper lip and dangling from its nose; from eyes made of resin hang strands of emerald beads that were likely meant to simulate tears. Holes in the mask were for threads used to attach it to grave wrappings that bound the body of the dead dignitary.

BEFORE AD 800	AD 800	AD 850

Vikings build the trading towns of Birka in Sweden and Hedeby in Denmark.

Swedish Vikings cross the Baltic Sea to establish trading posts in southern Finland and Lithuania. They then push deep into Russia and take over the Slavic settlement of Novgorod.

Charlemagne dies and leaves his empire to his son Louis the Pious.

The Vikings trade along the Dnieper and Volga rivers to bring goods to the Byzantine and Persian empires.

Norwegian and Danish Vikings fight each other for possession of the city of Dublin in Ireland.

Norwegians colonize Iceland.

Viking raiders penetrate as far south as the Mediterranean—reaching Spain and the city of Pisa in Italy.

Harald Fairhair initiates centralized rule over scattered settlements in Norway.

A Viking fleet, led by Sigfried and Orm, lays siege to Paris for almost a year.

Anglo-Saxon king Alfred of Wessex signs a treaty with the Danish leader Guthrum but still fortifies his kingdom against further Viking attacks.

AD 787 Danish Viking ships first appear on the coast of England.

AD 793 Vikings attack the monastery on the island of Lindisfarne off the coast of Northumbria.

NORTHERN EUROPE

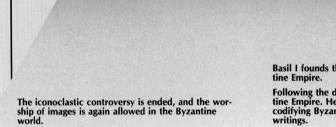

The iconoclastic controversy is ended, and the worship of images is again allowed in the Byzantine world.

Basil I founds the Macedonian dynasty of the Byzantine Empire.

Following the death of Basil, Leo VI rules the Byzantine Empire. He is given the name "the Wise," for codifying Byzantine laws and for his profound writings.

BYZANTIUM

Military campaigns are launched against the Ainu in the northern provinces.

Two Buddhist sects are introduced: the Tendai by the monk Saichō and the Shingon by the monk Kūkai.

Sugawara no Michizane emerges as a dominant figure in the Japanese government.

Japan breaks formal relations with China because of the political turmoil that accompanied the fall of the Tang dynasty.

AD 794 Emperor Kammu establishes a new capital at Heian-kyō, the modern city of Kyoto, which remains the center of Japanese government until 1185.

JAPAN

700 BC-AD 200 The Adena mound-building culture flourishes in the eastern woodlands of North America.

200 BC-AD 400 The Hopewell culture emerges in the Scioto River valley in southern Ohio and other areas of the eastern United States.

AD 300-900 The people of the Mogollon culture, in the mountainous regions of the southwest, fashion red ware and brown ware and live in pit houses.

AD 500-1000 The Tiahuanaco and Huari cultures in Peru reach their zenith.

AD 600 The Hohokam culture thrives in the southern Arizona desert.

AD 700 The Anasazi, a people who lived on the Colorado Plateau in the American west, begin to build pueblos.

800-1500 The Mississippian societies construct temple mounds and ceremonial centers across the eastern United States. The major center of Cahokia achieves its apex between 1050 and 1250.

THE AMERICAS

TimeFrame AD 800-1000

AD 900	AD 950	AD 1000

The Burgundian monastery of Cluny is founded.

Frankish king Charles the Simple cedes Norman land to Viking chieftain Rollo, in the treaty signed at St. Clair-sur-Epte.

Eirik the Red, having discovered Greenland in 981, sets sail for the island with about 450 people to establish a colony.

King Olaf I Tryggvason begins to rule over Norway.

Leif Eirikson, son of Eirik the Red, discovers the New World and winters there, perhaps at the site now called "L'Anse aux Meadows" in Newfoundland. He names his discovery Vinland.

The Fatimid caliphate is established in North Africa.

Trade treaties with Russia are ratified with Prince Oleg.

Romanus Lecapenus becomes regent for Constantine VII, then proclaims himself co-emperor in 920.

Constantine VII becomes sole emperor. He chronicles the history of his empire.

Nicephorus Phocas wrests Crete away from Arab control. He becomes emperor in 963 and reconquers Antioch and Aleppo in Syria.

After the six-year reign of John Tzimisces, Basil II takes over the Byzantine throne.

The Russians undergo conversion to Orthodox Christianity. Basil II gives his sister's hand in marriage to Prince Vladimir of Kiev.

The Pillow Book, by Lady Sei Shōnagon, and the romance novel *The Tale of Genji*, by Lady Murasaki Shikibu, are written. Both are literary masterpieces that give revealing accounts of court life.

The domination of the government by the Fujiwara clan reaches a peak under the leadership of Fujiwara no Michinaga.

900-1200 Tollan, in the Valley of Mexico, becomes the capital city of the Toltecs, a people known for their fine glazed pottery and large stone figures.

The Mogollon begin producing spectacular black and white Mimbres pottery.

BIBLIOGRAPHY

BOOKS

Almgren, Bertil, et al., *The Viking*. Gothenberg, Sweden: AB Nordbok, 1975.

Atkinson, Ian, *The Viking Ships*. Cambridge: Cambridge University Press, 1986.

Bainton, Roland H., and the Editors of Horizon Magazine, *The Horizon History of Christianity*. New York: American Heritage, 1964.

Baynes, Norman H., and H. St. L. B. Moss, eds., *Byzantium: An Introduction to East Roman Civilization*. London: Oxford University Press, 1948.

Beckwith, John, *Early Christian and Byzantine Art*. Harmondsworth, Middlesex, England: Penguin Books, 1970.

Bernal, Ignacio, *Great Sculpture of Ancient Mexico*, (Reynal's World History of Great Sculpture). New York: Reynal / William Morrow, 1979.

Borgen, Robert, *Sugawara no Michizane and the Early Heian Court*. Cambridge, Mass.: Council on East Asian Studies, Harvard University, 1986.

Branston, Brian, *Gods & Heroes from Viking Mythology*. New York: Schocken, 1978.

Brody, J. J., Catherine J. Scott, and Steven A. LeBlanc, *Mimbres Pottery: Ancient Art of the American Southwest*. New York: Hudson Hills Press / The American Federation of Arts, 1983.

Brøgger, A. W., and H. Shetelig, *Osebergfundet*. Vols. 1 and 2. Oslo: Universitetets Oldsaksamling, 1917.

Brøndsted, Johannes, *The Vikings*. Transl. by Kalle Skov. Harmondsworth, Middlesex, England: Penguin Books, 1986.

Bury, J. B.:
The Eastern Roman Empire. Vol. 4 of *The Cambridge Medieval History*. New York: Macmillan, 1927.
A History of the Eastern Roman Empire from the Fall of Irene to the Accession of Basil I. New York: Russell & Russell, 1965.

Bushnell, G. H. S., *Peru* (Ancient Peoples and Places series). New York: Frederick A. Praeger, 1963.

Christensen, Arne Emil, Jr., *Boats of the North: A History of Boatbuilding in Norway*. Oslo: Norske Samlaget, 1968.

Civardi, Anne, and James Graham-Campbell, *The Time Traveller Book of Viking Raiders*. London: Usborne Publishing Ltd., 1977.

Coe, Michael D., *Mexico*. London: Thames and Hudson, 1984.

Coe, Michael, Dean Snow, and Elizabeth Benson, *Atlas of Ancient America*. New York: Facts on File Publications, 1986.

Coedès, G., *The Making of South East Asia*. Transl. by H. M. Wright. London: Routledge & Kegan Paul, 1966.

The Columbia Lippincott Gazetteer of the World. Edited by Leon E. Seltzer. New York: Columbia University Press / J. B. Lippincott, 1962.

Crumlin-Pedersen, O., and R. Finch, *From Viking Ship to Victory*. London: Her Majesty's Stationery Office, 1977.

Davidson, H. R. Ellis, *Gods and Myths of Northern Europe*. Harmondsworth, Middlesex, England: Penguin Books, 1972.

Davies, Nigel, *The Ancient Kingdoms of Mexico*. Harmondsworth, Middlesex, England: Penguin Books, 1985.

Diehl, Richard A., *Tula: The Toltec Capital of Ancient Mexico*. London: Thames and Hudson, 1983.

Encyclopaedia Britannica. Vol. 12. Chicago: Encyclopaedia Britannica Inc., 1973.

Farrell, R. T., ed., *The Vikings*. London: Phillimore & Co., 1982.

Foote, Peter, and David M. Wilson, *The Viking Achievement*. London: Sidgwick & Jackson, 1973.

Foss, Clive, and Paul Magdalino, *The Making of the Past: Rome and Byzantium*. Oxford: Phaidon, 1977.

Franch, José Alcina, *Pre-Columbian Art*. Transl. by I. Mark Paris. New York: Harry N. Abrams, 1983.

Frere-Cook, Gervis, ed., *The Decorative Arts of the Mariner*. London: Jupiter Books, 1974.

Fukuyama, Toshio, *Heian Temples: Byodo-in and Chuson-ji*. Transl. by Ronald K. Jones. New York: Weatherhill, 1976.

Garraty, John A., and Peter Gay, eds., *The Columbia History of the World*. New York: Harper & Row, 1985.

Geijer, Agnes, *A History of Textile Art*. Totowa, N.J.: Pasold Research Fund / Sotheby Parke Bernet Publications, 1979.

Gibson, Michael, *The Vikings*. Morristown, N.J.: Silver Burdett, 1985.

Gladwin, Harold Sterling, *A History of the Ancient Southwest*. Portland, Maine: The Bond Wheelwright Co., 1957.

Graham-Campbell, James, *The Viking World*. London: Frances Lincoln / Weidenfeld & Nicholson, 1980.

Graham-Campbell, James, and Dafydd Kidd, *The Vikings*. London: British Museum Publications, 1980.

Hagen, Anders, *The Viking Ship Finds*. Oslo: Universitetets Oldsaksamling, 1966.

Hall, D. G. E., *A History of South-East Asia*. New York: St. Martin's Press, 1981.

Hall, John Whitney, *Japan: From Prehistory to Modern Times*. Tokyo: Charles E. Tuttle Co., 1971.

Hall, John W., and Jeffrey P. Mass, eds., *Medieval Japan: Essays in Institutional History*. New Haven, Conn.: Yale University Press, 1974.

Hall, Richard, *The Excavations at York: The Viking Dig*. London: The Bodley Head, 1984.

Haussig, H. W., *A History of Byzantine Civilization*. Transl. by J. M. Hussey. New York: Praeger, 1971.

Heath, Ian, and Angus McBride, *The Vikings*. London: Osprey, 1987.

Hempel, Rose, *The Heian Civilization of Japan*. Transl. by Katherine Watson. Oxford: Phaidon, 1983.

Hetherington, Paul, *Byzantium: City of Gold, City of Faith*. London: Orbis, 1983.

Hoffman, Alice S., *The Book of Sagas*. New York: E. P. Dutton, no date.

Holmqvist, Wilhelm, *Swedish Vikings on Helgo and Birka*. Stockholm: Swedish Booksellers Assoc., 1979.

Hughes, Sukey, *Washi: The World of Japanese Paper*. Tokyo: Kodansha International, 1978.

Ienaga, Saburo, *Painting in the Yamato Style*. Transl. by John M. Shields. New York: Weatherhill, 1973.

Ishida, Hisatoyo, *Esoteric Buddhist Painting*. Transl. by E. Dale Saunders. New York: Kodansha International Ltd. / USA Ltd., 1987.

Ishii, Ryōsuke, *A History of Political Institutions in Japan*. Tokyo: University of Tokyo Press, 1980.

Jacobs, David, and the Editors of Horizon Magazine, *Constantinople: City on the Golden Horn*. New York: American Heritage, 1969.

Jenkins, Romilly, *Byzantium: The Imperial Centuries A.D. 610-1071*. New York: Random House, 1966.

Jennings, Jesse D., ed., *Ancient Native Americans*. San Francisco: W. H. Freeman, 1978.

Jones, Gwyn, *A History of the Vikings*. New York: Oxford University Press, 1968.

Katz, Friedrich, *The Ancient American Civilizations*. Transl. by K. M. Lois Simpson. New York: Praeger, 1974.

Kazhdan, Alexander, and Giles Constable, *People and Power in Byzantium: An Introduction to Modern Byzantine Studies*. Washington, D.C.: Dumbarton Oaks Center for Byzantine Studies, Trustees for Harvard University, 1982.

Kirkby, Michael Hasloch, *The Vikings*. Oxford: Phaidon, 1977.

Kubler, George, *The Art and Architecture of Ancient America: The Mexican, Mayan and Andean Peoples*. Harmondsworth, Middlesex, England: Penguin Books, 1984.

Kucharek, Casimir, *The Byzantine-Slav Liturgy of St. John Chrysostom: Its Origin and Evolution*. Allendale, N.J.: Alleluia Press, 1971.

La Fay, Howard, *The Vikings*. Washington, D.C.: National Geographic Society, 1972.

Lazarides, Paul, *Hossios Loukas.* Athens: Apollo Editions, 1978.

Leonard, Jonathan Norton, and the Editors of Time-Life Books:
Ancient America (Great Ages of Man series). New York: Time Inc., 1967.
Early Japan (Great Ages of Man series). New York: Time-Life Books, 1976.

Liddell, Robert, *Byzantium and Istanbul.* London: Jonathan Cape, 1956.

Logan, F. Donald, *The Vikings in History.* Totowa, N.J.: Barnes & Noble, 1983.

Lu, David John, *Sources of Japanese History.* Vol. 1. New York: McGraw-Hill, 1974.

MacCulloch, John Arnott, *Eddic.* Vol. 2 of *The Mythology of All Races.* New York: Cooper Square Publishers, 1964.

Magnusson, Magnus, *Viking: Hammer of the North.* London: Orbis, 1985.

Mango, Cyril:
Byzantine Architecture. London: Faber and Faber / Electa Editrice, 1986.
Byzantium: The Empire of New Rome. London: Weidenfeld and Nicolson, 1980.

Meyer, Milton W., *Japan: A Concise History.* Boston, Mass.: Allyn and Bacon, 1966.

Miller, Mary Ellen, *The Art of Mesoamerica from Olmec to Aztec.* London: Thames and Hudson, 1986.

Morgan, William N., *Prehistoric Architecture in the Eastern United States.* Cambridge, Mass.: The MIT Press, 1980.

Morris, Ivan, *The World of the Shining Prince: Court Life in Ancient Japan.* New York: Alfred A. Knopf, 1964.

Morris, Ivan, ed. and transl., *The Pillow Book of Sei Shōnagon.* 2 vols. New York: Columbia University Press, 1967.

National Geographic Atlas of the World. Washington, D.C.: National Geographic Society, 1970.

Nickel, Heinrich L., *Byzantinische Kunst.* Heidelberg: Lambert Schneider, 1964.

Obolensky, Dimitri, *The Byzantine Commonwealth: Eastern Europe, 500-1453.* New York: Praeger, 1971.

Okudaira, Hideo, *Emaki: Japanese Picture Scrolls.* Rutland, Vt.: Charles E. Tuttle Co., 1962.

Olsen, Olaf, and Ole Crumlin-Pedersen, *Five Viking Ships from Roskilde Fjord.* Transl. by Barbara Bluestone. Copenhagen: The National Museum, 1985.

Ortiz, Alfonso, *Southwest.* Vol. 9 of *Handbook of North American Indians.* Washington, D.C.: Smithsonian Institution, 1979.

Ostrogorsky, George, *History of the Byzantine State.* Transl. by Joan Hussey. New Brunswick, N.J.: Rutgers University Press, 1969.

Page, R. I., *Runes: Reading the Past.* London: British Museum Publications, 1987.

Pálsson, Hermann, and Paul Edwards, transls., *Gautrek's Saga and Other Medieval Tales.* London: University of London Press, 1968.

Peoples and Places of the Past. Washington, D.C.: The National Geographic Society, 1983.

Pohl, Frederick J., *The Viking Settlements of North America.* New York: Clarkson N. Potter, 1972.

Rand McNally Atlas of the World. Chicago: Rand McNally, 1983.

Randsborg, Klavs, *The Viking Age in Denmark: The Formation of a State.* London: Gerald Duckworth & Co., 1980.

Reischauer, Edwin O., *Japan: Past and Present.* New York: Alfred A. Knopf, 1965.

Rice, David Talbot, *Art of the Byzantine Era.* London: Thames and Hudson, 1986.

Rice, David Talbot, ed., *The Dawn of European Civilization.* New York: McGraw-Hill, 1965.

Rice, Tamara Talbot, *Everyday Life in Byzantium.* London: B. T. Batsford, 1967.

Runciman, Steven:
Byzantine Civilisation. New York: Longmans, Green and Co., 1933.
Byzantine Style and Civilization. Harmondsworth, Middlesex, England: Penguin Books, 1975.

Sansom, George, *A History of Japan to 1334.* Stanford, Calif.: Stanford University Press, 1958.

Sawyer, P. H.:
The Age of the Vikings. New York: St. Martin's Press, 1972.
Kings and Vikings: Scandinavia and Europe AD 700-1100. London: Methuen, 1982.

Seckel, Dietrich, *Emakimono: The Art of the Japanese Painted Hand-Scroll.* Transl. by J. Maxwell Brownjohn. New York: Pantheon Books, 1959.

Sherrard, Philip, and the Editors of Time-Life Books, *Byzantium* (Great Ages of Man series). New York: Time-Life Books, 1975.

Shikibu, Murasaki, *The Tale of Genji.* Transl. by Edward G. Seidensticker. New York: Alfred A. Knopf, 1976.

Silverberg, Robert, *The Mound Builders.* Greenwich, Conn.: New York Graphic Society, 1970.

Simons, Gerald, and the Editors of Time-Life Books, *Barbarian Europe* (Great Ages of Man series). Alexandria, Va.: Time-Life Books, 1979.

Simpson, Jacqueline, *Everyday Life in the Viking Age.* New York: G. P. Putnam's Sons, 1967.

Sjøvold, Thorleif:
The Oseberg Find: And the Other Viking Ship Finds. Oslo: Universitetets Oldsaksamling, 1969.
The Viking Ships in Oslo. Oslo: Universitetets Oldsaksamling, 1985.

Smith, Bradley, *Japan: A History in Art.* Garden City, N.Y.: Doubleday, 1964.

Spencer, Robert F., et al., *The Native Americans: Ethnology and Backgrounds of the North American Indians.* New York: Harper & Row, 1977.

Stokstad, Marilyn, *Medieval Art.* New York: Harper & Row, 1986.

Terry, Patricia, transl., *Poems of the Vikings: The Elder Edda.* Indianapolis: Bobbs-Merrill, 1969.

Terukazu, Akiyama, *Treasures of Asia: Japanese Painting.* New York: Rizzoli International, 1977.

Varley, H. Paul, *Japanese Culture.* Honolulu: University of Hawaii Press, 1984.

Vasiliev, A. A., *History of the Byzantine Empire 324-1453.* Vol. 1. Madison, Wis.: University of Wisconsin Press, 1984.

Volbach, F., and Georges Duthuit, *Art Byzantin.* Paris: Les Éditions Albert Lévy, 1933.

Weaver, Muriel Porter, *The Aztecs, Maya, and Their Predecessors.* New York: Academic Press, 1981.

Weitzmann, Kurt, *Byzantine Liturgical Psalters and Gospels.* London: Variorum Reprints, 1980.

Weitzmann, Kurt, et al., *The Icon.* New York: Alfred A. Knopf, 1982.

Wernick, Robert, and the Editors of Time-Life Books, *The Vikings* (The Seafarers series). Alexandria, Va.: Time-Life Books, 1979.

Wessel, Klaus, *Byzantine Enamels: From the 5th to the 13th Century.* Transl. by Irene R. Gibbons. Greenwich, Conn.: New York Graphic Society, 1967.

Whitelock, Dorothy, David C. Douglas, and Susie I. Tucker, eds., *The Anglo-Saxon Chronicle.* Westport, Conn.: Greenwood Press, 1986.

Wilson, David M., *The Vikings and Their Origins.* London: Thames and Hudson, 1980.

Wilson, David M., ed., *The Northern World: The History and Heritage of Northern Europe AD 400-1100.* New York: Harry N. Abrams, 1980.

Wilson, David M., and Ole Klindt-Jensen, *Viking Art.* Ithaca, N.Y.: Cornell University Press, 1966.

Wise, Terence, *Saxon, Viking and Norman* (Men-At-Arms series). London: Osprey, 1981.

Wright, F. A., transl., *The Works of Liudprand of Cremona.* London: George Routledge & Sons, 1930.

Yanagi, Munemoto, et al., *Byzantium.* Transl. by Nicholas Fry. London: Cassel, 1978.

PERIODICALS

Haury, Emil W., "The Hohokam: First Masters of the American Desert." *National Geographic,* May 1967.

Stuart, George E., "Who Were the 'Mound Builders?' " *National Geographic,* December 1972.

Wilkerson, S. Jeffrey K., "Man's 80 Centuries in Veracruz." *National Geographic,* August 1980.

OTHER

A Thousand Cranes. Seattle / San Francisco: Seattle Art Museum, Chronicle Books, 1987.

Christensen, Arne Emil, *Guide to the Viking Ship Museum.* Oslo: Universitetets Oldsaksamling, 1984.

Crumlin-Pedersen, Ole, and Max Vinner, eds., *Sailing into the Past.* Transl. by Gillian Fellows Jensen, et al. Roskilde, Denmark: The Viking Ship Museum, 1986.

Dumbarton Oaks Papers. No. 18. Washington, D.C.: The Dumbarton Oaks Center for Byzantine Studies, Trustees for Harvard University, 1964.

Grierson, Philip, *Byzantine Coinage.* Washington, D.C.: Dumbarton Oaks, Trustees for Harvard University, 1982.

Hellenic Maritime Museum, museum catalog. Piraeus, Greece: Hellenic Maritime Museum, 1984.

Kyōtarō, Nishikawa, and Emily J. Sano, *The Great Age of Japanese Buddhist Sculpture AD 600-1300.* Fort Worth, Tex.: Kimbell Art Museum, 1982.

Murase, Miyeko, *Emaki: Narrative Scrolls from Japan.* Tokyo: The Asia Society with the Agency for Cultural Affairs, 1983.

The Treasury of San Marco Venice. Exhibit catalog, National Gallery of Art (New York). Milan: Olivetti, 1984.

Tweddle, Dominic, and Richard Hall, *Viking Ships.* York, England: Cultural Resource Management Ltd. / York Archaeological Trust, 1987.

Vikan, Gary, "Art, Medicine, and Magic in Early Byzantium." In *Dumbarton Oaks Papers.* No. 38. Washington, D.C.: Dumbarton Oaks Center for Byzantine Studies, 1984.

Vikan, Gary, ed., *Illuminated Greek Manuscripts from American Collections.* Exhibit catalog. Princeton, N.J.: The Art Museum, Princeton University, 1973.

Vikan, Gary, and John Nesbitt, *Security in Byzantium: Locking, Sealing and Weighing.* Washington, D.C.: Dumbarton Oaks Center for Byzantine Studies, 1980.

PICTURE CREDITS

ACKNOWLEDGMENTS

The following materials have been reprinted with the kind permission of the publishers: Pages 17-18 and page 19: "The Sibyl's Prophecy" and "The Lay of Vafthrudnir" from *Poems of the Vikings,* translated by Patricia Terry, New York: Macmillan Publishing Co., © 1969. Throughout chapter 3: Phrases and poems of Sugawara no Michizane from *Sugawara no Michizane and the Early Heian Court,* by Robert Borgen, Cambridge, Mass.: Council on East Asian Studies, Harvard University, © 1986. Phrases and verses of Sei Shōnagon from *The Pillow Book of Sei Shōnagon,* translated by Ivan Morris, Vols. 1 and 2, New York: Columbia University Press, © 1967.

The editors also wish to thank the following individuals and institutions for their valuable assistance in the preparation of this volume:

England: Cambridge—R. I. Page, Elrington and Bosworth Professor of Anglo-Saxon, University of Cambridge. London—James Graham-Campbell, Reader in Medieval Archaeololgy, University College; Victor Harris, Department of Oriental Antiquities, British Museum; Lyn Rodley, Society for Hellenic Studies; Joe Roome, Science Museum; Lawrence Smith, Department of Oriental Antiquities, British Museum.

Federal Republic of Germany: Berlin—Dieter Eisleb, Direktor, Museum für Völkerkunde, Staatliche Museen Preussischer Kulturbesitz; Heidi Klein, Bildarchiv Preussischer Kulturbesitz; Hans-Georg Severin, Direktor, Frühchristlich-Byzantinische Abteilung, Staatliche Museen Preussischer Kulturbesitz. Cologne—Gisela Völger, Direktor, Rautenstrauch-Joest Museum für Völkerkunde; Irmgard Weigmann, Erzbischöfliches Diözesan Museum; Karin von Welck, Rautenstrauch-Joest Museum für Völkerkunde. Hamburg—Rose Hempel, Museum für Kunst und Gewerbe. Munich—Ferdinand Anton; Irmgard Ernstmeier, Hirmer Verlag. Neumünster—Erich Gockel, Karl Wachholtz Verlag. Schleswig—Christian Radtke, Archäologisches Landesmuseum; Stuttgart—Klaus-J. Brandt, Linden Museum; Ursula Didoni, Linden Museum.

France: Lyon—Monique Jay, Librarian and Chief, Picture Archives, Musée Historique des Tissus. Paris—François Avril, Curateur, Département des Manuscrits, Bibliothèque Nationale; Christophe Barbotin, Conservateur du Département des Antiquités Egyptiennes, Musée du Louvre; Pascale Barthélemy, Curateur, Département des Manuscrits, Bibliothèque Nationale; Laure Beaumont-Maillet, Conservateur en Chef du Cabinet des Estampes, Bibliothèque Nationale; Catherine Bélanger, Chargée des Relations Extérieures du Musée du Louvre; Jeannette Chalufour, Archives Tallandier; Béatrice Coti, Directrice du Service Iconographique, Éditions Mazenod; Antoinette Decaudin, Documentaliste, Département des Antiquités Orientales, Musée du Louvre; Michel Fleury, Président de la IV Section de l'École Pratique des Hautes Études; Marie-Odile Germain, Conservateur, Département de Manuscrits, Bibliothèque Nationale; Marie-Françoise Huygues des Étages, Conservateur, Musée de la Marine; Françoise Jestaz, Conservateur, Cabinet des Estampes, Bibliothèque Nationale; Marie Montembault, Documentaliste, Département des Antiquités Grecques et Romaines, Musée du Louvre; Marie-Odile Roy, Service Photographique, Bibliothèque Nationale; Jacqueline Sanson, Conservateur, Directeur du Service Photographique, Bibliothèque Nationale.

German Democratic Republic: Berlin—Arne Effenberger, Direktor, Frühchristlich-Byzantinische Sammlung, Staatliche Museen zu Berlin.

Italy: Florence—Brigitte Baumbusch, Scala. Milan—Luisa Ricciarini, Agenzia Ricciarini. Rome—Graeme Barker, Director, British School at Rome; Kiyo Hosino, Librarian, Istituto Giapponese di Cultura.

Japan: Tokyo—J. Edward Kidder, International Christian University; Mari Koide, Tokyo National Museum; Machiko Morita, Tokyo National Museum.

Spain: Madrid—Biblioteca Nacional.

Sweden: Gothenburg—Gunnar Stenmar, Publisher, AB Nordbok.

U.S.A.: Alabama: Tuscaloosa—Richard A. Diehl, Chairman, Department of Anthropology, University of Alabama. Colorado: Durango—Linda Martin, Chapin Mesa Archaeological Museum, Mesa Verde National Park. Illinois: Collinsville—Bill Iseminger, Site Interpreter, Cahokia Mounds Historic Site. Kansas: Manhattan—Patricia J. O'Brien, Department of Anthropology, Kansas State University. Oklahoma: Tulsa—Frederick Myers, Thomas Gilcrease Institute of American History and Art; Edwin Wade, Philbrook Museum of Art. Tennessee: Knoxville—Jefferson Chapman, Curator of Archaeology and Professor, Department of Anthropology, University of Tennessee. Washington, D.C.—William Loerke, Professor of Byzantine Art, Dumbarton Oaks, and Visiting Professor, History of Architecture, Catholic University of America; Catherine Tkacz, Dumbarton Oaks.

INDEX